IMAGES of America
EAST ATLANTA

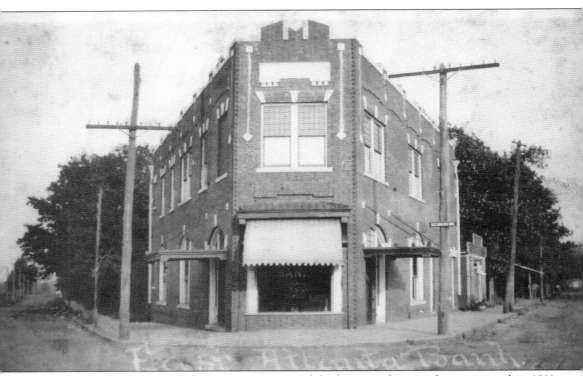

The East Atlanta Bank became a mainstay of the business district when it opened in 1911 at the southeast corner of Flat Shoals and Glenwood Avenues. Today, it is still the most iconic and recognizable building in the area. (Courtesy of the Everitt family.)

ON THE COVER: Pioneer J.W. McWilliams opened his general store at the northwest corner of the well-traveled intersection of Glenwood and Flat Shoals Avenues on Thanksgiving Day, 1891. His first sale was a pound of coffee. In 1892, the store became East Atlanta's first post office and McWilliams became its first postmaster. This photograph was taken in 1906. (Courtesy of Mary Frances Banks.)

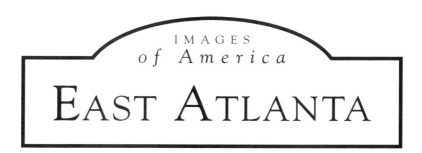

IMAGES *of America*
EAST ATLANTA

Henry Bryant and Katina VanCronkhite

ARCADIA
PUBLISHING

Copyright © 2014 by Henry Bryant and Katina VanCronkhite
ISBN 978-1-4671-1121-8

Published by Arcadia Publishing
Charleston, South Carolina

Printed in the United States of America

Library of Congress Control Number: 2013941692

For all general information, please contact Arcadia Publishing:
Telephone 843-853-2070
Fax 843-853-0044
E-mail sales@arcadiapublishing.com
For customer service and orders:
Toll-Free 1-888-313-2665

Visit us on the Internet at www.arcadiapublishing.com

This book is dedicated to the leaders and visionaries of the East Atlanta Community Association—past and present—who believe in East Atlanta's future.

Contents

Acknowledgments		6
Introduction		7
1.	Early Settlement and Civil War	9
2.	From Battleground to Village	25
3.	Thriving and Surviving	53
4.	World War II and the Boom	75
5.	Divided by the Interstate and Integration	101
6.	Rebuilding Together	113
Bibliography		127

Acknowledgments

Writing a book that documents the history of a community is impossible without the story keepers and storytellers who hold the past close to their hearts and guard it for the future. Dozens of East Atlanta families and pioneer descendants shared their history and memorabilia with us. Even though we could not include all of the photographs and stories they entrusted to us, what they shared innately became part of this book.

We want to express our deepest appreciation to those who endured our repeated visits, phone calls, and e-mails to help us paint a more accurate history of East Atlanta through the decades: Robert Argoe, Louis Arnold, Evelyn Bailey, Mary Frances Banks, Marion Blackwell, Katherine Carter, Steve Clarke, Bill and Beth Crabill, Bill and Janice Elliott, Ina Evans, the Everitt family, David Floyd, James Hackney, Mary Ann Hightower, Martha Ann Holmes, Louise Howington, E.C. Knox, Tom Lindsey Jr., Sandra Moody, Jennifer Murray and Mark Dobiecki, the Murphy family, the Pattillo family, Jimmy Jones, Dennis Taylor and the Sylvester Cemetery Association, W.L. Wagnon Jr., and the Williams family.

Thanks to the many individuals, families, and organizations who shared images: the Atlanta Fulton Public Library System, the Atlanta Independent School System, the Battle of Atlanta Commemoration Organization (BATL), Courtney Bryant, Ann Lee Bussey, Connie Callaway Cook, the DeKalb County Public Library, Plemon El-Amin, First Iconium Baptist Church, Winn Smith Floyd, the Georgia Department of Transportation, Lynn Giglio, YMCA of Metro Atlanta, Sherwood Harrington, the Indianapolis Motor Speedway, Michael Knight, Mark Lin, the Mosby family, Phil Northman, Pentrex Media Group, Catherine Perry, Dorothy Rose, Sam Sox Jr., Allyn Stewart, Genie Strickland, Claudia Stucke, Frank Tippens, Traveler's Rest Baptist Church, David VanCronkhite, Kristin Vanderpool, Krissy Venneman, the Waldrip family, Hugh M. Walker, and Wesley Woods Senior Living.

We are grateful to the Martha Brown United Methodist Church archives, a treasure trove of East Atlanta's early history. Thanks also to Jill Sweetapple at the DeKalb History Center and to the archivists at the Atlanta History Center, the Georgia State University Special Collections, and the Georgia Archives for their assistance.

And great thanks to our editor, Liz Gurley, and all the Arcadia Publishing staff who agreed that East Atlanta's story should be told.

INTRODUCTION

East Atlanta is a state of mind. If you feel like you live there, then you do.

—Natalia Holton
East Atlanta Community Association president, 1988

East Atlanta has never been easy to describe, and the borders have been especially difficult to pinpoint. Its boundaries and characteristics have changed as frequently as the decades. Ultimately, East Atlanta is an experience as much as a place—the sum of its land and the people who labored to inhabit it.

The area has always been a desirable land rich in natural resources. Early geological events left creeks, shoals, and rivers near the crest of a soapstone ridge. The native people made quarries to mine the soapstone and created artifacts that were traded as far north as the Great Lakes. A layer of granite extends under the fertile soil from Stone Mountain throughout the area. By 1733, when the first colonists arrived, the Native Americans in Georgia had divided themselves into a Confederation of Creek tribes and the Cherokee Nation, setting the first regional boundary separating the two factions at the Chattahoochee River. The high ground through East Atlanta was the Creek Indian Sandtown-Flat Shoals Trail, part of a larger trading route connecting the coast with the Chattahoochee River by way of Panola Shoals, on the South River.

In 1811, the Creeks, who had been ceding portions of their ancestral territory to the growing white population, officially barred further land cessation. The Creeks and the Cherokees allied with the British in the short-lived War of 1812, but both were soon to lose their ancestral lands. In the Indian Springs Treaty of 1821, Creek chief McIntosh ceded the land that would eventually become 10 new counties, including DeKalb, to the United States.

The whole of the Native American territory was divided into land lots, which were given away in lotteries to veterans of the Revolutionary War and the War of 1812 as well as to longtime Georgia citizens. The original two land lots of East Atlanta were lots number 176 and 177. James "Spanish Jim" Brown arrived in the area around the same time as the railroad that was laid along the Hightower (Etowah) Trail with Atlanta as its terminus. The 202.5 acres in Land Lot 177 were bounded by what are now Moreland Avenue, Memorial Drive, Eastside Avenue, and Glenwood Avenue. Land Lot 176 is a similar square of land directly to the south of Glenwood. Both land lots are bisected diagonally by the old Indian trail.

Before the Civil War, white settlers established their own roads, some along the old routes and some new ones connecting area mills and plantations. By 1860, James Brown had acquired the southern half of Land Lot 177. After the Civil War, he and his wife, Nancy Terry Brown, became the first to settle on the land, founding the East Atlanta community. In 1870, he purchased the northern half of the land lot. James M. Calhoun, Atlanta's Civil War mayor, was among those who recognized the value of the land, establishing his country plantation in the western half of

Land Lot 176. After the war, Gov. Joseph E. Brown acquired Calhoun's property as part of his many landholdings. The Brown family developed it as Brownwood Park in the 1920s.

During the Civil War, the old Indian trail became the location of the Union front lines, with a major cannon emplacement near the intersection of Middle McDonough (Flat Shoals) and Magazine (Glenwood) Roads. The Battle of Atlanta began in East Atlanta in the early afternoon of July 22, 1864, and was fought largely in the Sugar Creek valley, across the two-to-three-square-mile battlefield. By the end of the day, 8,500 Confederate soldiers and 3,600 Union soldiers lay dead, including Union general James B. McPherson and Confederate general W.H.T. Walker. Modern historians sometimes refer to the fight as the "Battle of Interstate 20" because the interstate was built in the Sugar Creek floodplain.

After the war, a little frame house was built near the Flat Shoals and Glenwood trails as a resting place for tired travelers. Freed-slave tenant farmers first met here in 1876 and founded Traveler's Rest Baptist Church, with a cemetery in the churchyard. In 1877, a monument to General McPherson was erected at his death site, attracting tourists and developers. In the 1880s, a new streetcar line was laid out adjacent to Flat Shoals Avenue and ending at Glennwood Avenue (then spelled with two ns). Soon, outlying farmers stopped at the east Atlanta crossroads to trade at the new stores that had sprung up there. By 1892, when the East Atlanta post office was placed in the McWilliams store, the name of the area changed from being a direction to being a destination with a capital *E*.

The 1891 McPherson Park subdivision brought families who desired good schools and fire and police protection. In 1910, the East Atlanta suburb voted to be annexed by the city and became an Atlanta neighborhood, providing these amenities. The neighborhood's official boundaries were Eastside Avenue to the east and the edge of the Joseph E. Brown family's property to the south. But East Atlanta also included the area west of Moreland and north of Glenwood to Entrenchment Creek (the Beltline area). Others just outside these boundaries claimed to live in East Atlanta, too. Along Flat Shoals, the boundary stretched farther north, not stopping at Moreland Avenue or Fair Street (Memorial Drive) but reaching to the edge of Reynoldstown, a freed-slave community near the railroad tracks.

East Atlanta celebrated the arrival of streetlights along the old Indian trail 65 years after soldiers dug in along Flat Shoals Avenue. Later, Moreland Avenue was paved to Macon and a new bridge over Sugar Creek connected Glenwood Avenue to the East Lake Golf Club.

During the Great Depression and World War II, East Atlanta businesses, banks, and neighbors rallied for each other. As soldiers returned home, most of the area's farms became part of the postwar housing boom. In the 1950s, a new library, new schools, and many new ranch-style homes added a mid-century bustle to the community. More annexation by Atlanta soon stretched East Atlanta's boundaries to Fayetteville Road.

In the 1960s, Interstate 20 severed the streets in the northern end of the community. This, combined with the legislated end of racial segregation for schools, public facilities, and housing, changed neighborhood dynamics. White flight battered the area, and, by the 1980s, it was bad enough to be filmed for a Chuck Norris movie needing blighted scenery. A new 1976 Atlanta Charter created Neighborhood Planning Unit-W, instigating the formation of the East Atlanta Community Association and again setting new boundaries. Interstate 20 became the northern boundary, while Moreland Avenue and the city limits remained the western, southern, and eastern edges.

As pioneering residents and merchants in the 1980s and 1990s reinvigorated the aging houses and shops, the neighborhood earned labels such as "the epitome of cool," attracting visitors from across metropolitan Atlanta and beyond. What began centuries ago as a promising land without borders continues to foster a boundless spirit of creativity and acceptance in a community where a brighter day is always dawning. And those living both inside and outside of the physical boundaries still stubbornly stake their claim to the East Atlanta experience.

One

Early Settlement and Civil War

From a time of geological upheaval, a land of attractive natural features and abundant resources was born. The land that is now East Atlanta was first the hunting grounds and trails of the Creek Native American people. Their major east-west trail, the Sandtown-Hightower Trail, crossed the Peachtree Trail at what became Five Points in downtown Atlanta. The Sandtown Trail high ground became East Atlanta's main road, Flat Shoals Avenue.

After a treaty was signed in 1821, the Creeks were removed to the Oklahoma Territory and their lands were given to longtime American citizens through land lotteries. These first settlers established plantations and farms, leaving other lots of land vacant and wooded. The railroads arrived in the 1840s, following the old Indian trails and high ground, with crossings only a mile north of East Atlanta. Before that, the DeKalb County seat, Decatur, was founded to the east, and then Terminus—later renamed Atlanta—was founded to the west.

The Battle of Atlanta began here shortly after 12:00 p.m. on July 22, 1864. The Union army set up its front lines strategically along the high ground in East Atlanta, opposite the Confederate fortifications of the city. The Union goal was to cut the rail lines on the east side by ripping up four miles of track between Moreland Avenue and Decatur. After a daring all-night march, the Confederate army attacked in East Atlanta. The soldiers battled intensely over Leggett's Hill, on Flat Shoals Avenue along Sugar Creek. When the fight was over at sundown, the area had been devastated, and 12,000 soldiers, including two generals, were dead.

The outcome of the battle led to the reelection of Pres. Abraham Lincoln and sealed the fate of the Confederacy. Afterward, Gen. William Sherman's army cut the remaining rail lines, laid siege to the city of Atlanta until it surrendered, and then began their legendary March to the Sea. But the good land and waters of East Atlanta were left intact, ripe for the rebuilding of a new economy and a new way of life.

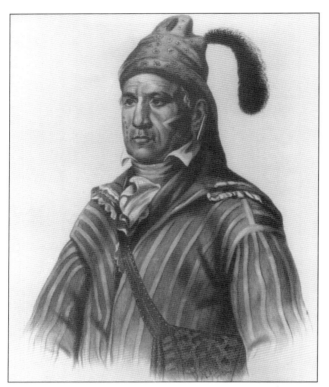

Menawa was a Muscogee Creek Indian chief who opposed the cessation of Indian lands to Georgia in the 1820s. He led an attack in 1825 that killed Chief William McIntosh, who signed the Treaty of Indian Springs and accepted relocation west of the Mississippi River without the approval of the Creek National Council. Menawa sought the reversal of the treaty in Washington but came home disappointed. (Courtesy of the Library of Congress.)

This bronze plaque shows the major trade routes of the Cherokee and Creek Indians, including the Flat Shoals and Sandtown Trails, which would become the major roads for white settlers. The plaque was placed in 1932 on the steps leading to the old DeKalb County Courthouse by the Campfire Girls, who had researched the trails with the assistance of E.A. Minor, a prominent East Atlanta resident. (Photograph by Katina VanCronkhite.)

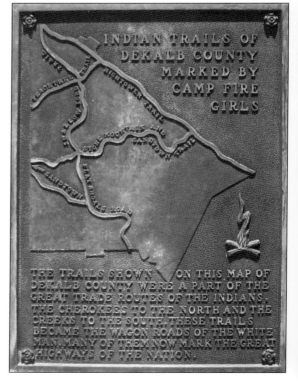

Early East Atlanta pioneer James Brown received the nickname of "Spanish Jim" because of a glass eye that he sometimes covered with a black patch. He moved to the area around 1842, and, by 1865, he owned all of Land Lot 177. Throughout his life, he bought and sold real estate in the area, farmed, and practiced his trade as a carpenter. (Courtesy of Mary Frances Banks.)

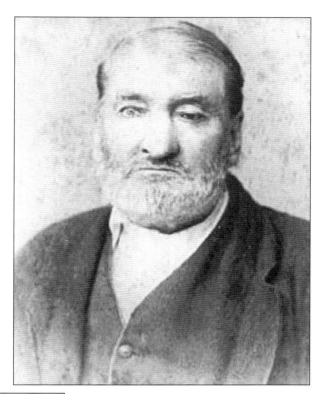

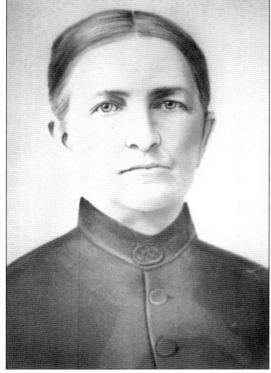

Nancy Terry married James Brown in about 1836. They moved to the area to be near her widowed mother, Ellen Terry, who had married Thomas Simmons, the owner of a gristmill and sawmill on Sugar Creek. When Simmons died in 1842, Ellen and her oldest son, Thomas Terry, ran the farm and the mills. When Thomas was murdered in 1861, his wife, Mary Jane, took over the mills. (Courtesy of Mary Frances Banks.)

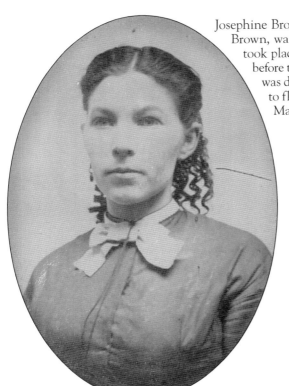

Josephine Brown, a daughter of James and Nancy Terry Brown, was 12 years old when the Battle of Atlanta took place. It is likely that the family fled the area before the battle began. Their home caught fire and was destroyed when Confederates fired cannons to flush out Union sharpshooters. (Courtesy of Mary Frances Banks.)

John W. McWilliams was a frequent visitor to the Browns' home before the war. He enlisted in the 42nd Georgia Regiment and fought in the Battle of Atlanta, near his home. McWilliams married Josephine Brown four years later. (Courtesy of Mary Frances Banks.)

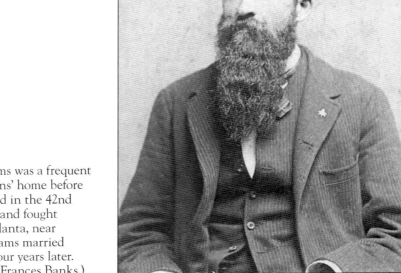

Another Brown daughter, Elizabeth Jane, married Confederate veteran John McKee. In 1877, McKee guided soldiers from the McPherson barracks on Peters Street in Atlanta to the exact spot of General McPherson's death to determine where a monument should be placed to honor him. (Courtesy of Mary Frances Banks.)

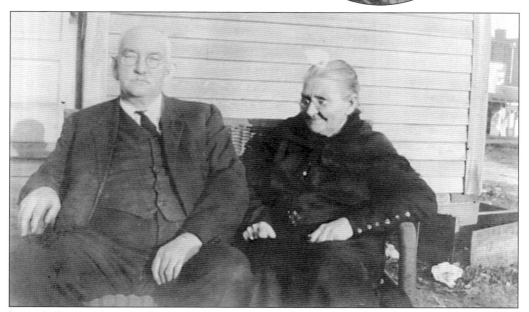

James F. Brown, the son of James and Nancy Brown, became one of the first businessmen in the area. He owned two retail and dry goods stores, one in Inman Park and the other in Cabbagetown. Brown and his sister Josephine McWilliams sat for this photograph near the McWilliams store in 1924, a year before Josephine died. (Courtesy of Mary Frances Banks.)

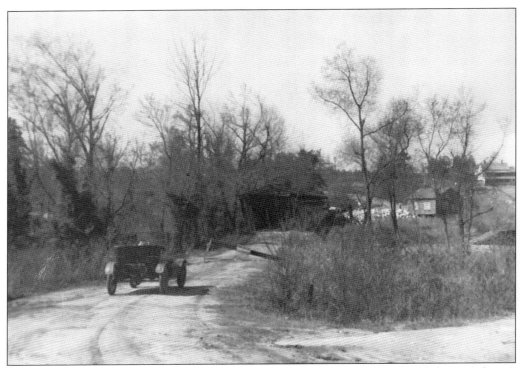

Flat Shoals Avenue in East Atlanta was named for the granite shoals in the South River, Atlanta's "other" river. After leaving the shoals, it flows into a major river system that reaches the Atlantic Ocean at Brunswick, Georgia. This is the road over the shoals, where DeKalb County's first and last covered bridge crossed the river. (Courtesy of the DeKalb County Public Library.)

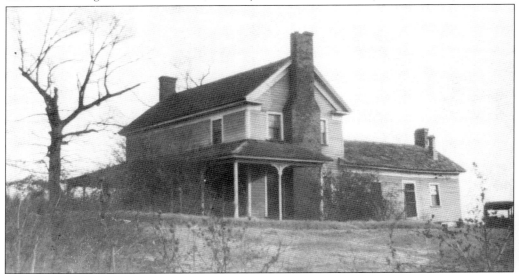

William Cobb owned a farm and gristmill south of Atlanta on Entrenchment Creek. At dawn on the day of the Battle of Atlanta, Gen. William J. Hardee's disoriented Confederate forces arrived at Cobb's Mill and procured him as a guide into East Atlanta to surprise Union forces. (Courtesy of Kenan Research Center at the Atlanta History Center.)

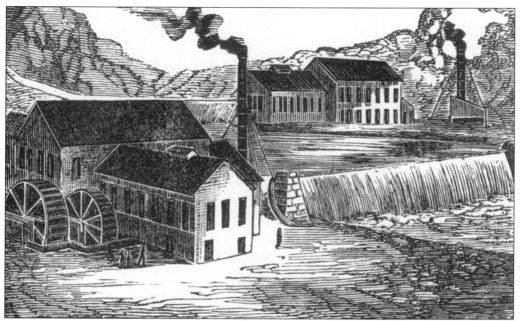

In 1863, Atlanta became a major paper-manufacturing center. Because of a desperate shortage of paper, the government funded the Sugar Creek Mills, five miles east of the city on the road to Soapstone Ridge (now Bouldercrest Drive). The mill ceased production in 1900 when it burned down in a fire caused by defective wiring. (From *Illustrated History of Atlanta* by Edward Young Clarke; courtesy of Special Collections of the DeKalb County Public Library.)

Well into the 1950s, East Atlanta residents recall playing and picnicking among the ruins of the old "Scully's Mill." These paper mill remains, photographed in the 1930s, are probably among those that were still seen in the 1960s behind the new Walker High School, which was named for Confederate general W.H.T. Walker and later renamed for DeKalb County astronaut Dr. Ronald McNair. (Courtesy of Kenan Research Center at the Atlanta History Center.)

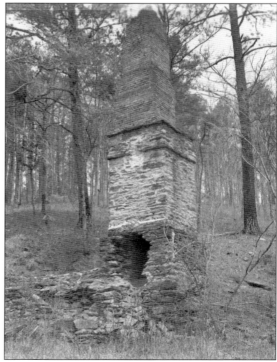

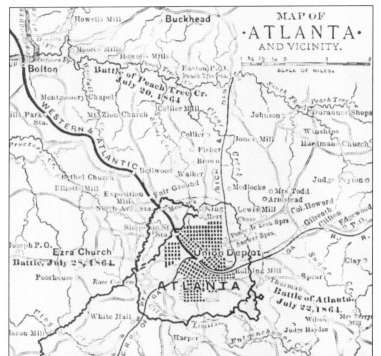

Col. Lemuel P. Grant, chief engineer of the Confederate Department of Georgia, began fortifying Atlanta after the fall of Vicksburg in July 1863. This map, made by US Corps of Engineers in 1864 after the Battle of Atlanta, shows the scope of his fortifications and the eastern area where most of the fighting occurred. (Courtesy of the Library of Congress.)

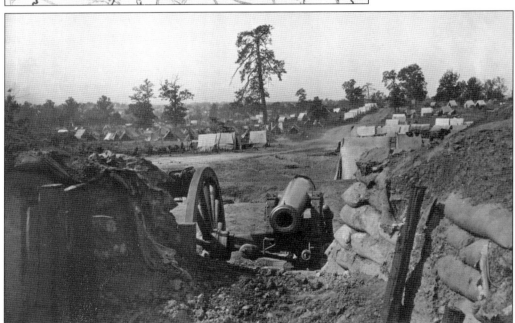

By 1864, Atlanta had become the strategic center of Confederate supply. Union commander general William Tecumseh Sherman believed Atlanta must be crushed, but he realized storming its 10-mile circle of fortifications was suicidal. Thus, the Battle of Atlanta was eventually fought beyond the city's outermost limits. The fortifications were never breached, but, with its railroad lines cut, Atlanta surrendered after two months of incessant bombing. (Courtesy of the Library of Congress.)

Under Gens. William T. Sherman and James B. McPherson, Gen. Francis P. Blair commanded the XVII Corps and ordered the taking of the Bald Hill promontory in East Atlanta one day before the Battle of Atlanta. His troops fiercely held the lines in East Atlanta until, in a strategic move, they withdrew to the hill and swung north and east, effectively closing the door on the Confederates late in the day. (Courtesy of the Library of Congress.)

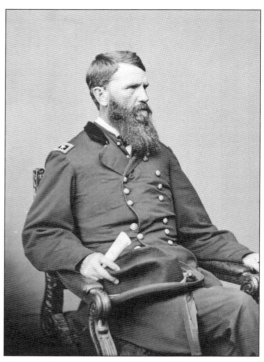

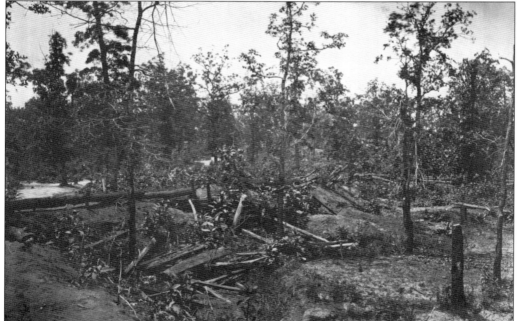

This photograph of the Battle of Atlanta entrenchments may well have been taken along Flat Shoals Avenue in East Atlanta. Soldiers dug in with picks and shovels, felled trees, and ripped apart area houses and barns to provide cover for their line of battle. The Battle of Atlanta was fought in this sparsely populated area two miles east of the city center. (Courtesy of the Library of Congress.)

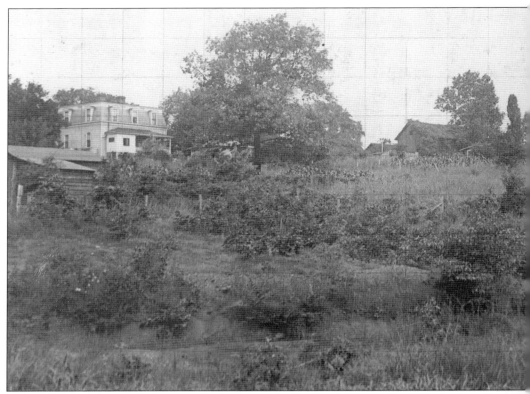

Bald Hill was a strategic high ground and prize in the Battle of Atlanta. In 1864, the Jesse Spear house was atop the hill, and soldiers used a spyglass to scan the area into downtown Atlanta. The hill was bulldozed during the construction of Interstate 20 in the late 1950s. This 1927 view

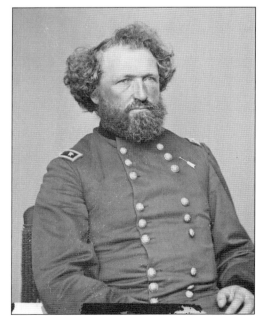

Gen. Mortimer Leggett commanded the Union forces that took Bald Hill on July 21, 1864. Forever after, the site was called Leggett's Hill, even by Atlantans. For a time, Flat Shoals Avenue was even renamed Leggett's Avenue. After the hill fell, Union forces moved from Decatur into the Confederate trenches in East Atlanta. Decatur, which had fallen earlier, had already become the Union supply center. (Courtesy of the Library of Congress.)

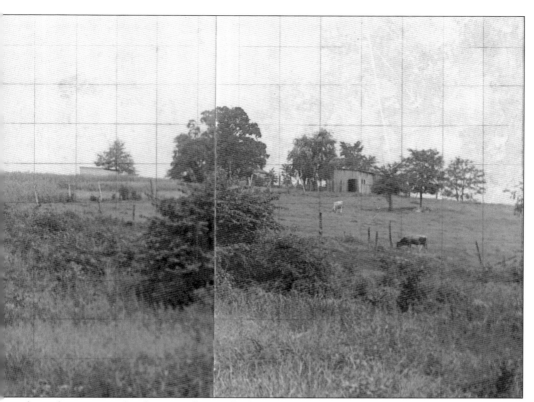

is from the east on what became the roadbed and shows the home and outbuildings of Frederick Koch. (Courtesy of Kenan Research Center at the Atlanta History Center.)

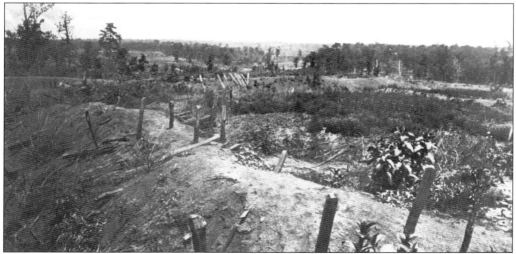

This view is purportedly of the outer defenses east of Atlanta, possibly near Leggett's Hill. Much of the area that was not wooded was farmland with fields of wheat, corn, and cotton. As Leggett's Hill fell, the Confederate outer works became the Union front lines, and the guns were turned to face Atlanta's center. (Courtesy of the Library of Congress.)

Union general James Birdseye McPherson was the dashing 35-year-old commander of the Army of the Tennessee, which was named for the river in Ohio. At the war's start, the Ohio native was engineering the Alcatraz fortress in San Francisco, but he quickly rose through the ranks in the fighting before 1864. He had requested leave to wed, but General Sherman asked him to postpone until Atlanta's capture. (Courtesy of the Library of Congress.)

On the morning of July 22, 1864, General McPherson reviewed troop positions in East Atlanta and determined that reinforcements were needed. At noon, while he was lunching with his generals a mile north at the railroad, the Battle of Atlanta began near Memorial Drive and Clifton Street. McPherson immediately rode toward the action. Hearing more gunfire on Flat Shoals Avenue, he traveled the wagon road below toward it. (Courtesy of the Library of Congress.)

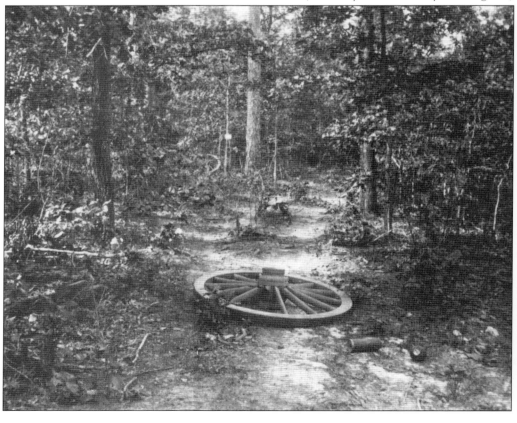

As General McPherson, accompanied by an orderly, reached a large pine, they were surprised by a Confederate unit that ordered them to halt. McPherson did, but, a moment later, he looked north over his shoulder, wheeled on his horse, and gave it the boot. Shots rang out, and the general fell, fatally wounded. His watch hit a rock and stopped at 2:02 p.m. (Courtesy of the Library of Congress.)

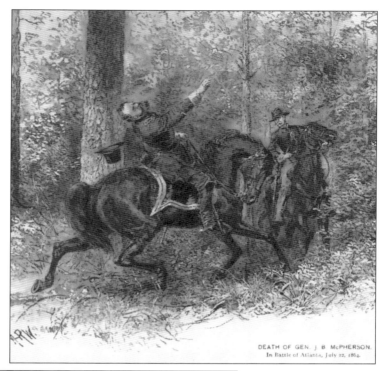

DEATH OF GEN. J. B. McPHERSON.
In Battle of Atlanta, July 22, 1864.

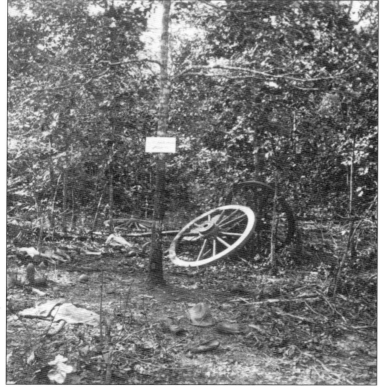

The historic battlefield photographs of the site of McPherson's death were taken by George Barnard on September 3, 1864, the day after the surrender of Atlanta. Gen. Andrew Hickenlooper, a McPherson friend, gathered the photographer and McPherson's orderly to visit the fresh field of battle. He nailed a small sign to mark the spot where the beloved general had died. (Courtesy of the Library of Congress.)

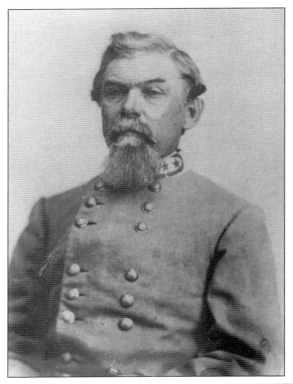

On July 20, Georgia's Gen. William J. Hardee and Confederate forces had experienced a tentative defeat at Peachtree Creek, north of Atlanta. Their new commander, Gen. John Bell Hood, had orders from Richmond to "take the fight to the enemy," and he ordered them on a 15-mile march around the southeast side of Atlanta to attack at dawn. They were delayed by exhaustion, confusion, and the conditions in the South River valley. (Courtesy of the Library of Congress.)

Born in County Cork, Ireland, Gen. Patrick Cleburne became a naturalized US citizen by 1860 and sided with the South because of the favorable treatment he received there as an immigrant. In 1864, to solve his army's manpower crisis, he proposed granting freedom to slaves in exchange for military service. Cleburne played a major role in attempting to turn away Sherman in East Atlanta. (Courtesy of the Library of Congress.)

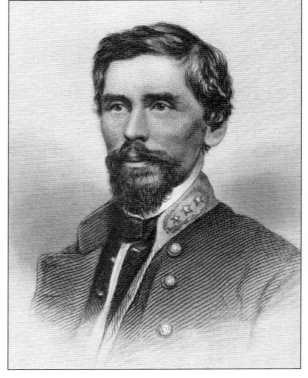

Peter Vertrees, a free black man from Tennessee, served as a medical assistant alongside his Confederate white uncle Dr. John L. Vertrees in the Orphan Brigade, 6th Kentucky Infantry, during the Battle of Atlanta. He later became a respected educator and pastor in Tennessee. In 1976, his granddaughter Ina Evans, who lived in East Atlanta, became the first African American woman to serve on the Atlanta School Board. (Courtesy of Ina Evans.)

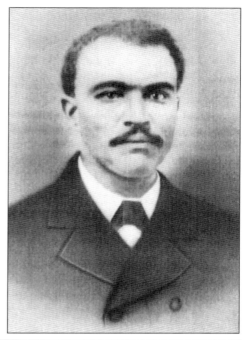

The map below, created for the centennial of the Battle of Atlanta, shows the neighborhood streets overlaid with an oval representing the battlefield. The dashed lines are the Union front lines, from Glenwood Avenue in East Atlanta to Copenhill, now the Carter Center. The arrows from the east are Union reinforcements, while the arrows from the south and west represent the Confederate attack. (Courtesy of the Georgia Department of Transportation.)

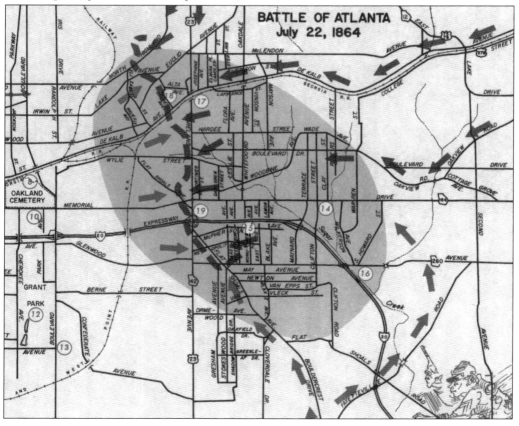

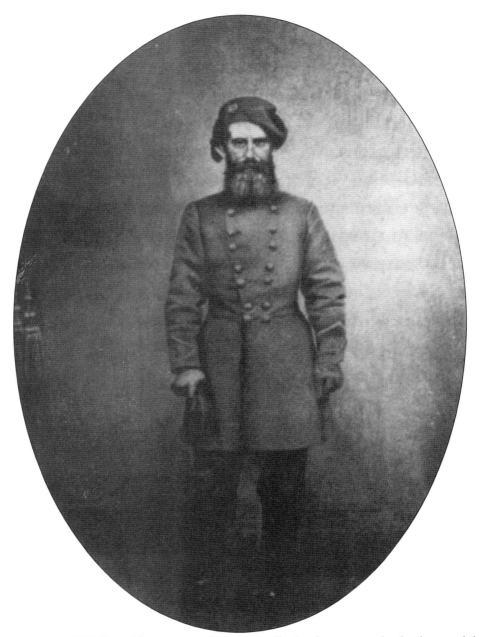

Maj. Gen. W.H.T. Walker told a correspondent that he "had rather receive the death wound than see Atlanta surrendered without contesting every inch of ground for its possession." A career soldier, Walker was a native of Augusta, Georgia, and the son of a former US senator. In 1864, he was 56 years old and had suffered so many previous injuries in battles that he was called "Old Shotpouch." After an all-night march, he was faced with crossing the 39-acre Terry millpond. As his troops were mired in the backwater, Walker rode ahead and was shot and killed by a sniper as he crossed Sugar Creek. His body was taken to the home of Mary Jane Terry, the widow of Thomas Terry, and then sent home to Augusta. Gen. William B. Bate continued the attack after Walker's death. (Courtesy of Hugh M. Walker.)

Two

From Battleground to Village

Resilience was the trademark of the pioneers who survived the war and returned to settle the area once again. Within 15 years of the Battle of Atlanta, farsighted businessmen envisioned a future of streetcars and a new suburban development. The Victorian homes and Craftsman bungalows of McPherson Park soon surrounded General McPherson's monument. East Atlanta became the home of merchants and tradesman from Atlanta as well as farmers, dairymen, blacksmiths, and railroad workers.

Seeing the steady flow of travelers into resurging Atlanta along the busy Flat Shoals thoroughfare, enterprising men like J.W. McWilliams, E.A. Minor, and Luther Marbut established their mercantile stores, creating a foundation for the community to grow. In 1896, there were only around 300 people in East Atlanta, but others soon followed with a desire to build a community with good schools, places of worship, and civic organizations.

Though change was everywhere, the remains of war were still very much evident. The entrenchment built along Flat Shoals and Glenwood Avenues in 1864 was still visible behind the East Atlanta Pharmacy when Dr. E.F. Fincher drove the first car in East Atlanta, scattering barking dogs and spooking horses. Bodies that had been quickly buried after the battle on Leggett's Hill were sporadically uncovered during plowing and cultivating seasons on the Koch farm and then removed for proper burials in the Marietta National Cemetery. After 1902, aging Civil War veterans and their families traveled on the new trolley line through East Atlanta to the new Confederate Soldiers' Home on Confederate Avenue.

In 1909, the City of Atlanta annexed East Atlanta, and commercial development began to steadily increase. A new local bank in 1911 and a thriving business district generated additional residential developments and the building of a new brick schoolhouse for the burgeoning school-age population. The early promotional advertisements that declared East Atlanta one of the "most delightful places of residence to be found with a bright mercantile and professional future" became a reality.

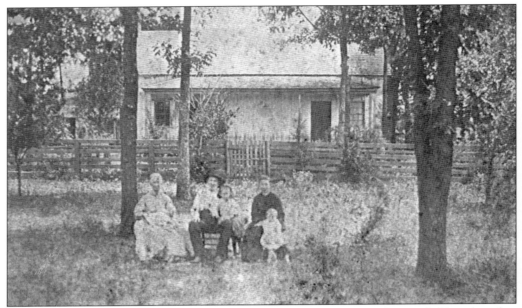

Above, James "Spanish Jim" Brown (center) and his wife, Nancy Terry Brown (left), gathered in 1885 with family members in front of their home, the first one built in Land Lot 177. The home is believed to have been located near Moreland and Flat Shoals Avenues. Nancy died in this house in 1889, and James followed in 1893. In May 1877, Brown sold a 30-foot-by-30-foot plot and a right-of-way to it from Flat Shoals Avenue to Capt. John R. McGinness of the McPherson Barracks for $1. The plot became the site of a monument memorializing General McPherson's death in the Battle of Atlanta. As seen below, soldiers obtained a decommissioned cannon, Stone Mountain granite, and Civil War rifle barrels for the fence corners, erecting the monument by September 1877. (Above, courtesy of Mary Frances Banks; below, courtesy of the DeKalb History Center.)

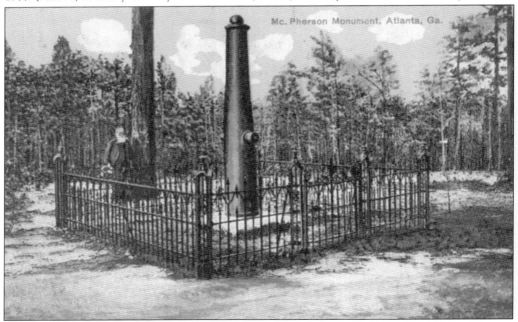

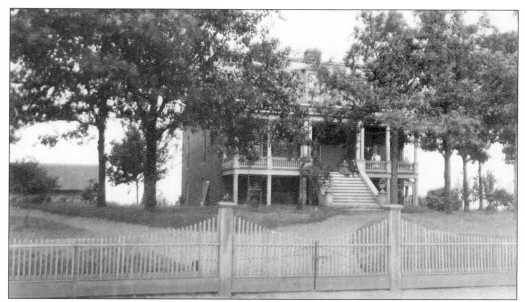

Frederick Koch, a gentleman farmer, built this home in 1879 on the top of Leggett's Hill, at the intersection of Flat Shoals and Moreland Avenues. The Koch family lived there until 1946. Afterward, it was used for various purposes until it was sold for the Interstate 20 right-of-way in 1958. German artists who painted the Atlanta Cyclorama came to Atlanta to make sketches for the Battle of Atlanta painting. Each day, they traveled by streetcar from their downtown hotel to the Koch house, where they had stored their supplies, and then walked north on Moreland Avenue to the railroad tracks to climb the scaffolding erected to view the terrain. Below, they are painting the Battle of Chickamauga back in their Wisconsin studio. (Both courtesy of Kenan Research Center at the Atlanta History Center.)

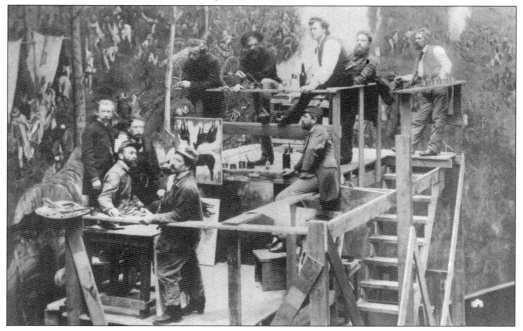

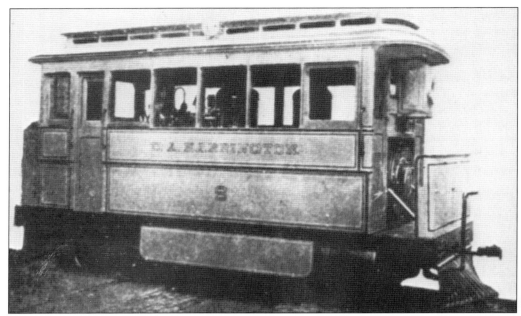

East Atlanta began suburban development with the arrival of the Metropolitan Street Railway, and many local streets still bear the names of early railway investors and directors, including Haas, Patterson, Moreland, and Brown. The railway began operation in 1883 with horse- and mule-drawn cars, adding coal-burning steam "dummy" cars (above) in 1887, which chugged and belched soot as they rolled along at 20 miles per hour. The line from downtown split at Faith's Crossing on Flat Shoals Avenue, just north of Fair Street (Memorial Drive), with one route continuing to Decatur and the other going through East Atlanta. After all of Atlanta's street railway lines were electrified in 1894, the dummies were sold. The map below outlines the original route of the Metropolitan Street Railroad Company. (Both courtesy of Pentrex Media Group.)

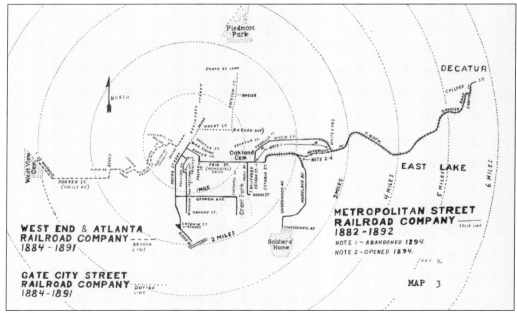

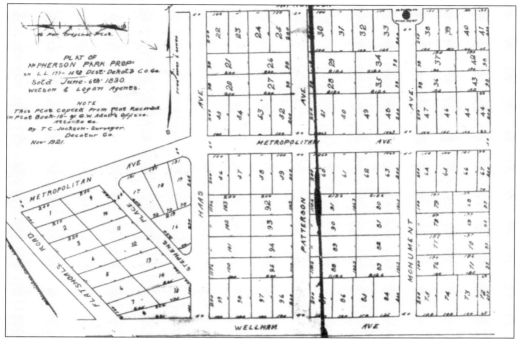

The 1890 plat of the McPherson Park subdivision shows large lots and a grid pattern of streets laid out around the existing McPherson Monument. The southern boundary was named for company president Thomas Wellham but was later renamed Glennwood after Atlanta's prominent Glenn family. The first home built in the subdivision was the house below, at 1346 Metropolitan Avenue. The original Victorian structure was altered around 1920 with Craftsman-style detailing, as seen in this 2007 photograph. (Both courtesy of Henry Bryant.)

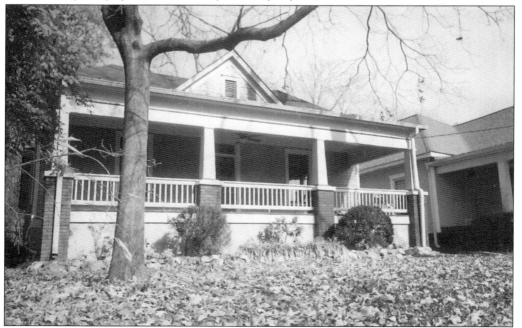

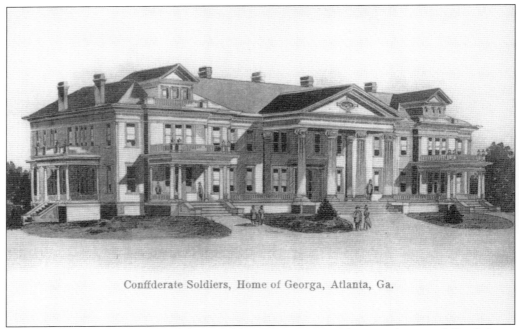

Conffederate Soldiers, Home of Georga, Atlanta, Ga.

The final destination of the Confederate Soldiers' Home streetcar line was the second Confederate Soldiers' Home, built in 1902 west of East Atlanta. It became a popular destination for neighborhood boys who liked to roller-skate on the concrete-floored pavilion later added on its front lawn. The boys tried to ease their uphill return trip to East Atlanta by grabbing the handles of the streetcar and being pulled on their skates up the hill to Moreland Avenue until being discovered by the conductor. Below, the Blue and Gray Association held a convention of Union and Confederate veterans in Atlanta in 1900. Many came by streetcar and walked the two blocks from Moreland and Flat Shoals Avenues to gather at the McPherson Monument. (Both courtesy of Katina VanCronkhite.)

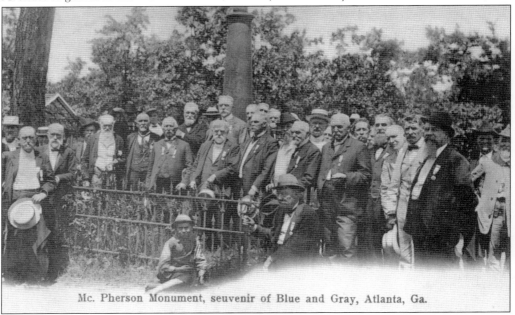

Mc. Pherson Monument, souvenir of Blue and Gray, Atlanta, Ga.

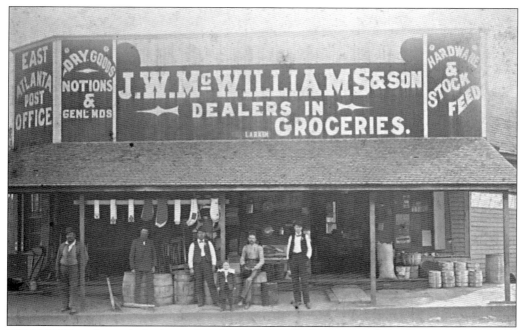

J.W. McWilliams's wood-plank merchandise store was the beginning of the East Atlanta business section. The store offered general merchandise, notions, hardware, groceries, and stock feed and boasted of a well and a watering trough, which were landmarks through the mid-1920s. East Atlanta's first post office and one of the area's first telephones were located here. Mules were corralled behind the store and used for delivery wagons. Below, Sam McWilliams (behind the counter) ran the store with his father and became the second postmaster in 1895. The boy in the rear of this 1896 photograph is his son Thomas Ernest McWilliams, who remained postmaster until his death in 1940. J.W. McWilliams died in 1934 at the age of 90. (Both courtesy of Mary Frances Banks.)

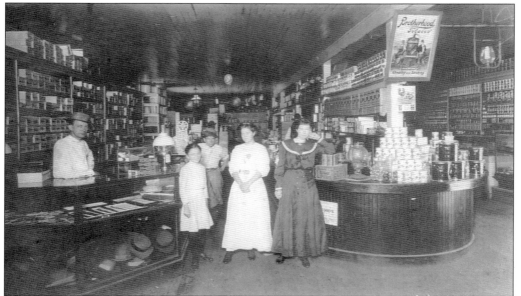

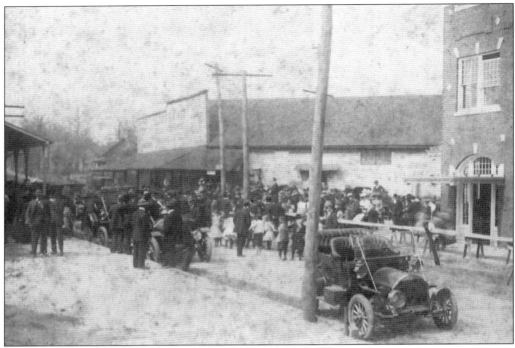

Marbut & Minor, seen in the center of the photograph above, became the second-largest grocery in the South and offered a vast array of goods. Founded by L.L. Marbut and E.A. Minor, the business opened across from the J.W. McWilliams store in 1896 as a small, three-cornered storefront. This photograph was taken at the 1911 opening of the East Atlanta Bank (right), looking north at the intersection of Flat Shoals and Glenwood Avenues. (Both courtesy of the Everitt family.)

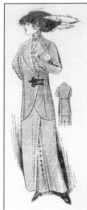

Marbut & Minor
Wholesale and Retail
General Merchandise
East Atlanta, Georgia

Staple Dry Goods and Notions,
Shoes for the Entire Family
The Newest Novelties
and all the Staples

Our styles are up-to-the-minute. Lead the procession for public favor.

Ladies'
Tailored
Suits and
Skirts
Millinery
Dress Wool-
ens and
Silks
Muslin
Underwear

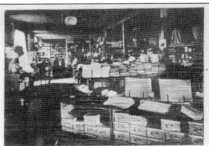

DRY GOODS DEPARTMENT

Groceries, Stock Feed, Field and
Garden Seed, Fresh Meats
and Hardware

Buckeye Incubators, and Poultry
Supplies

Gasoline for sale at lowest
price at all times

Marbut & Minor
PHONE 2251
East Atlanta, Ga.

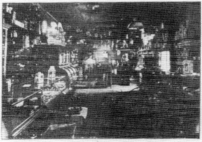

INTERIOR GROCERY DEPARTMENT

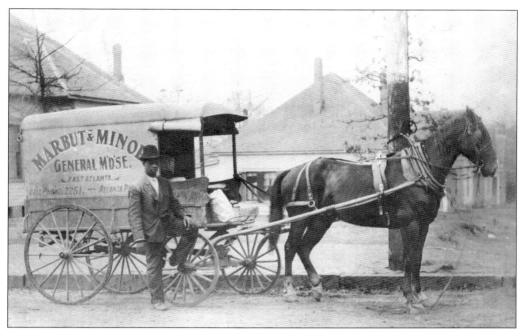

Marbut & Minor delivery wagons, such as the one above with an unidentified driver, were familiar sights on the streets of East Atlanta. Many neighborhood boys found their first jobs there. Charlie Everitt began his long grocery career in East Atlanta as a 12-year-old delivery boy in 1906, when his father, Charles B. Everitt, was manager. The store (below) sold goods ordered by the freight-car loads and produce that was grown at the Marbut & Minor truck farm, near Clifton Street and Glenwood Avenue. (Both courtesy of the Everitt family.)

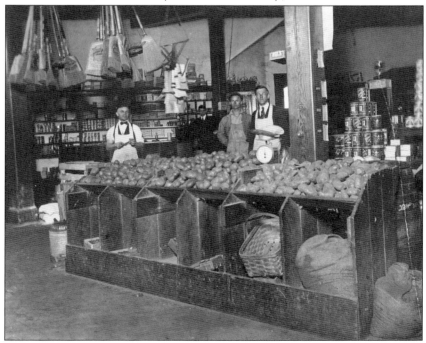

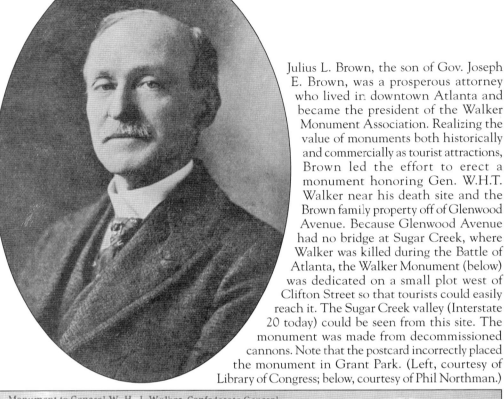

Julius L. Brown, the son of Gov. Joseph E. Brown, was a prosperous attorney who lived in downtown Atlanta and became the president of the Walker Monument Association. Realizing the value of monuments both historically and commercially as tourist attractions, Brown led the effort to erect a monument honoring Gen. W.H.T. Walker near his death site and the Brown family property off of Glenwood Avenue. Because Glenwood Avenue had no bridge at Sugar Creek, where Walker was killed during the Battle of Atlanta, the Walker Monument (below) was dedicated on a small plot west of Clifton Street so that tourists could easily reach it. The Sugar Creek valley (Interstate 20 today) could be seen from this site. The monument was made from decommissioned cannons. Note that the postcard incorrectly placed the monument in Grant Park. (Left, courtesy of Library of Congress; below, courtesy of Phil Northman.)

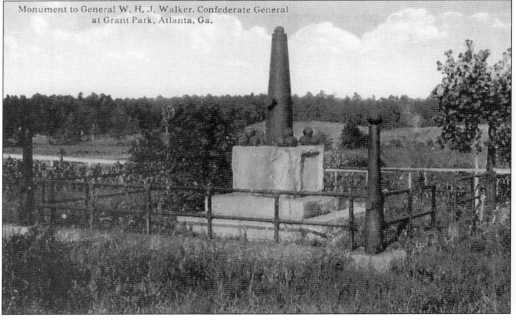

Monument to General W. H. J. Walker, Confederate General at Grant Park, Atlanta, Ga.

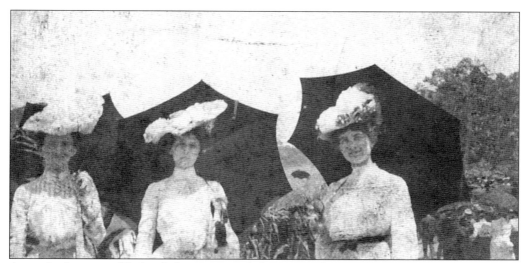

A parade of carriages filled with dignitaries, including Gov. Allen Candler, traveled from the Kimball House Hotel in downtown Atlanta for the dedication and unveiling of the Walker Monument on July 22, 1902. After the ceremonies, Gertrude McWilliams, Maude McWilliams, and one of the Marbut daughters joined the large crowd gathered in Brownwood Park, where enough barbecue to feed 2,000 guests had been prepared. (Courtesy of Mary Frances Banks.)

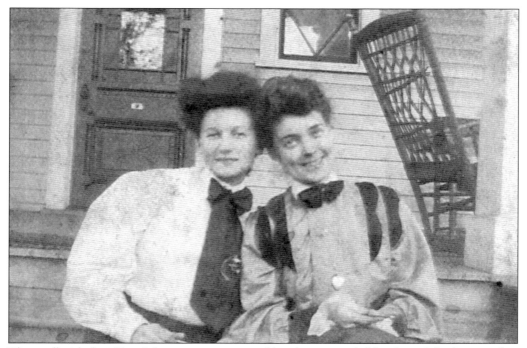

The small, tight-knit East Atlanta community was like a large extended family, and the front porches of homes were frequent destinations. Here, Maude David (left) visits with Maude McWilliams on the McWilliams front porch around 1900. (Courtesy of Mary Frances Banks.)

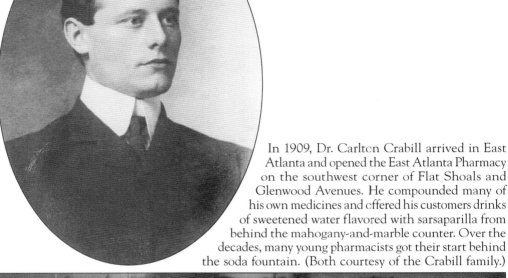

In 1909, Dr. Carlton Crabill arrived in East Atlanta and opened the East Atlanta Pharmacy on the southwest corner of Flat Shoals and Glenwood Avenues. He compounded many of his own medicines and offered his customers drinks of sweetened water flavored with sarsaparilla from behind the mahogany-and-marble counter. Over the decades, many young pharmacists got their start behind the soda fountain. (Both courtesy of the Crabill family.)

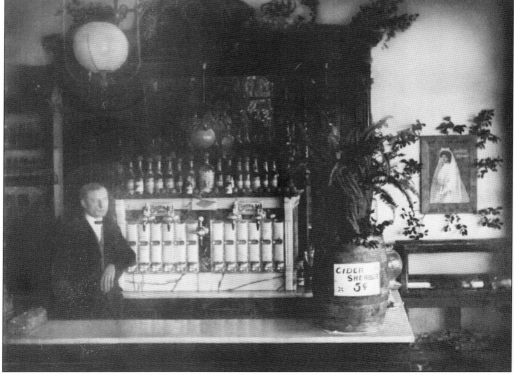

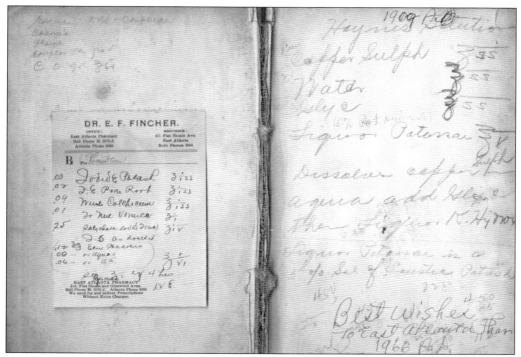

Dr. Crabill started his compound-drug–formula book in 1909 and passed it on to Dr. Charles W. Hill when he took over as pharmacist. Carlton "Bill" Crabill Jr. then received the book when he became pharmacist. The prescription for rheumatism relief in the book was written by Dr. E.F. Fincher, a longtime neighborhood physician who had an office at the pharmacy. (Courtesy of the Crabill family.)

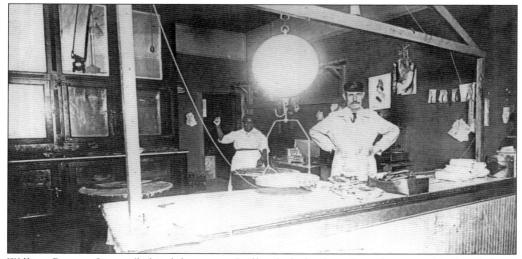

William Bartow Owens (behind the counter) offered wholesale and retail meats at his East Atlanta Market, at 500 Flat Shoals Avenue, in 1910. With three daughters, Owens's invitation to bachelor pharmacist Carlton Crabill to board with his family on Metropolitan Avenue may have been a well-calculated move. Crabill eventually married Owens's daughter Trudie. (Courtesy of Martha Brown United Methodist Church.)

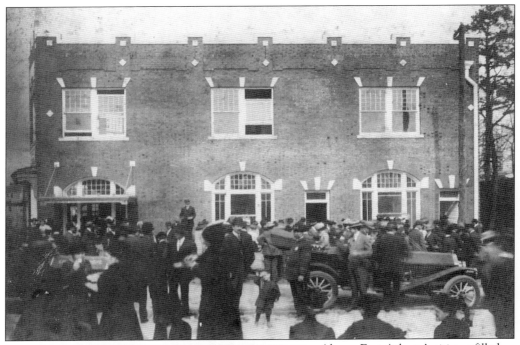

Above, East Atlanta's citizens filled Flat Shoals Avenue during the opening of the East Atlanta Bank in 1911. The founders realized that farmers traveling to Atlanta would instead stop in East Atlanta for feed and seed loans at reasonable rates. The bank set up scales to weigh commodities at harvest time and offered fair payment. The brick building, with its unusual stone accents and stone-capped crenelated parapet, remains an architectural jewel in the neighborhood. (Courtesy of the Everitt family.)

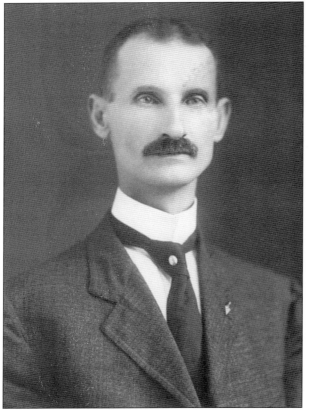

Ebenezer Augustus "E.A." Minor was one of the most well-known and well-respected names in the area. He cofounded the Marbut & Minor mercantile store and served as president and director of the East Atlanta Bank. The East Atlanta Masonic Lodge was named in his honor—reportedly the only Masonic lodge named for a living person at that time. (Courtesy of the Everitt family.)

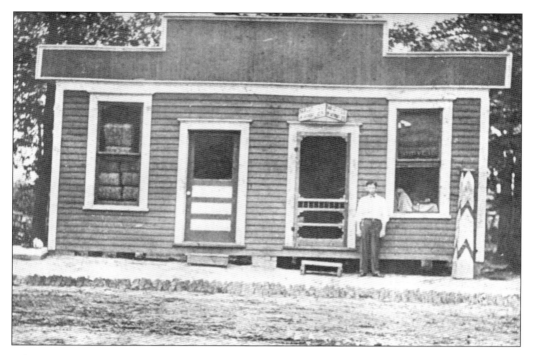

John Carlton Fallin opened his East Atlanta Barber Shop (above) by 1913 along Flat Shoals Avenue. Fallin (below, far left) was one of several barbers who, along with a shoe shine boy, made the barbershop a regular habit and a popular social stop for local men. (Both courtesy of Martha Brown United Methodist Church.)

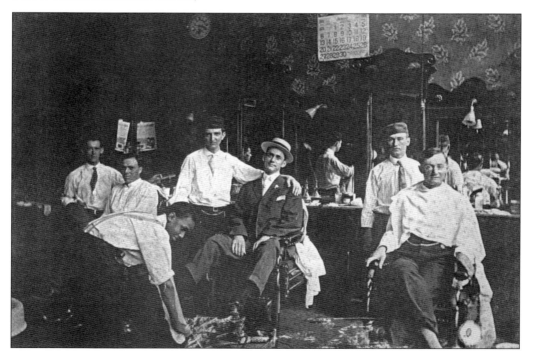

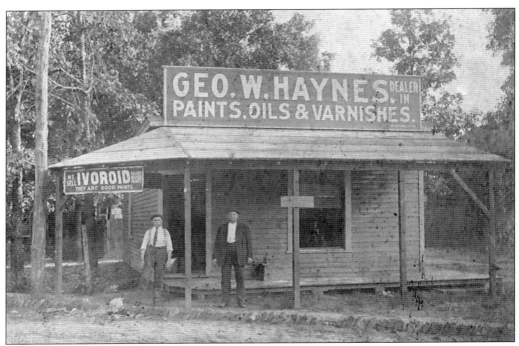

George Washington Haynes, seen above standing to the right of his brother William, established his paint store on the corner of Flat Shoals and May Avenues. Also a carpenter, he built his home (below) on an adjoining lot on May Avenue. His wife, Martha, stands with their children on the porch of their Victorian-style cottage in 1908. They are, from left to right, George Jr., Lena, Myrta, and Alton. (Both courtesy of Donald Stephen Clarke.)

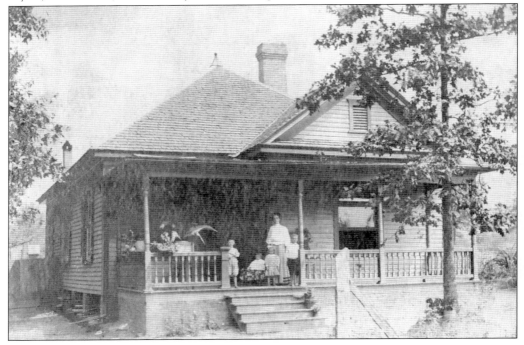

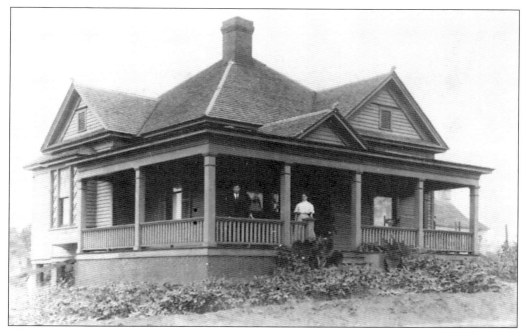

This Queen Anne cottage was built at 453 Haas Avenue by 1910. It was among the first homes constructed on the street, which was named after Aaron Haas, one of the founders of the Metropolitan Streetcar Railway Company. (Courtesy of Allyn Stewart.)

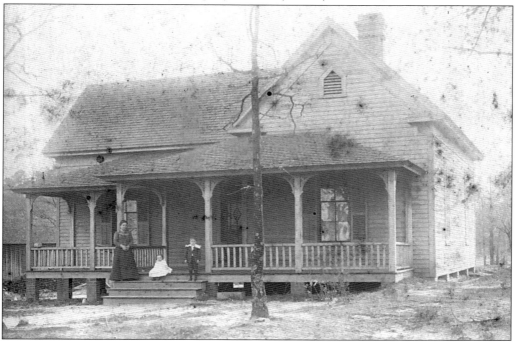

Several members of the McWilliams clan lived in the 400 block of Flat Shoals Avenue, which is now the East Atlanta Village. This is one of their homes, which was built in the popular single-gabled style with a generous front porch featuring gingerbread trim. (Courtesy of Mary Frances Banks.)

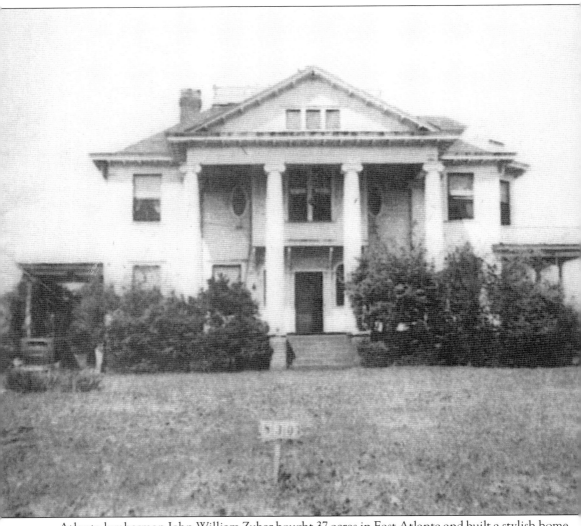

Atlanta lumberman John William Zuber bought 37 acres in East Atlanta and built a stylish home on the property in 1906 for his new bride, Gertie Rogers of Chattanooga. Zuber's father, a German immigrant who fought in the Civil War with a New York regiment, witnessed the destruction of Atlanta and moved his family here in 1871 to help rebuild. He founded a wholesale lumber business that John, his oldest son, later took over. John and Gertie Zuber raised four children, including a set of twins, in the two-story, wood-frame mansion. The home reflects Zuber's knowledge of fine woods, materials, and craftsmanship. Located about half a mile from East Atlanta Village, it is currently the only structure in East Atlanta listed in the National Register of Historic Places. The home is an example of the Neoclassical Revival style that was popular at that time, with a large portico, ionic columns, a wraparound porch on the right, and a porte cochere on the left. (Courtesy of Jennifer Murray and Marc Dobiecki.)

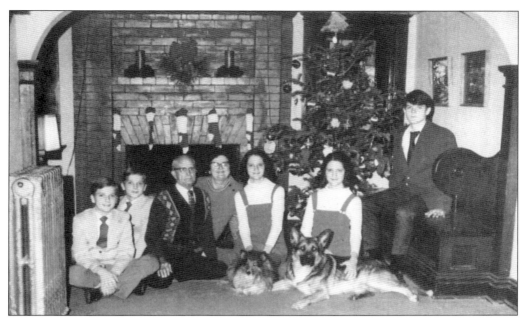

John M. Jarrell, an engineer with the Southern Railroad, purchased the Zuber home in 1937 and brought his new wife, Martha Frances Mitchell, there in 1954. The Jarrells had five children, including two sets of identical twins. At Christmas, they placed their tree in the two-story, birch-paneled entry hall under the grand staircase landing. The Jarrell family lived in the home for 66 years. Today, the Zuber-Jarrell House is situated on only two acres of land. Current owners Jennifer Murray and Marc Dobiecki bought it in 2003 from Martha Jarrell and have meticulously restored and maintained the landmark home. The 2009 photograph below shows the newly restored columns, porch, and leaded glass. (Both courtesy of Jennifer Murray and Marc Dobiecki.)

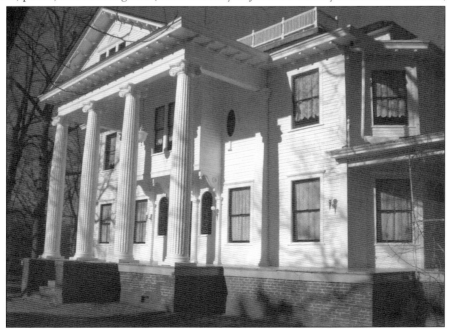

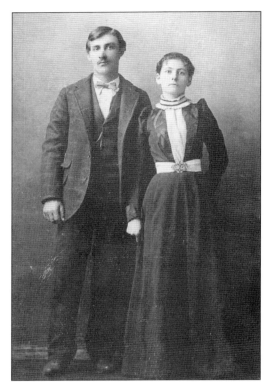

The opportunities that came with affordable land and jobs around East Atlanta attracted farmers, dairymen, and laborers as well as merchants. Frank Armstrong immigrated to America from Bohemia with his aunt and uncle when he was six. He eventually settled in the East Atlanta area, where he became a farmer and dairyman and married Emma Hallie Wilson in 1897. (Courtesy of Sandra Moody.)

Mark Minor, the younger brother of E.A. Minor, began one of the South's two tie factories in his home on Flat Shoals Avenue. The house had once been the meeting place of East Atlanta Methodist Church (later Martha Brown United Methodist Church) in 1892, and all of Minor's family became prominent in the history of the church. His sister Vashti married Charles B. Everitt, a manager at Marbut & Minor. (Courtesy of the Everitt family.)

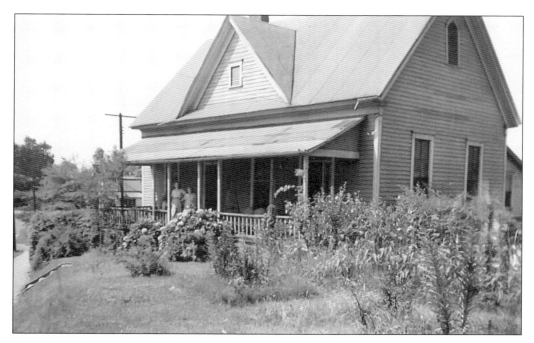

In 1894, the McPherson Park Company sold the triangle-shaped piece of land at the corner of Haas Avenue and Stephens Place (now Metropolitan Place) for $1 to the trustees of the new East Atlanta School, who included J.W. McWilliams, James F. Brown, and McPherson Park Company president J. Thomas Wellham. The schoolhouse is seen above in the 1930s, after it had been converted into a home with a front porch and a kitchen at the rear. Below, a Professor Jarell (back row, with hat) oversaw the small school when this photograph was taken around 1900. (Above, courtesy of E.C. Knox; below, courtesy of Mary Frances Banks.)

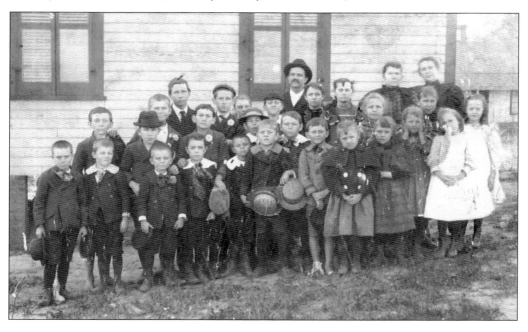

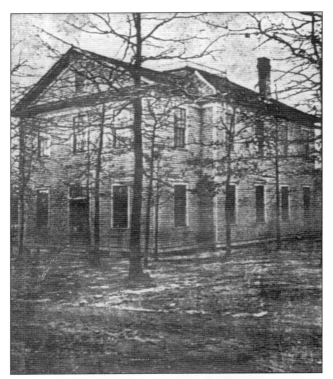

The next school building was built around 1905 at the corner of Metropolitan and Patterson Avenues. The McPherson Park Company sold the land for $10 with the condition that a schoolhouse costing not less than $2,000 be built within two years. The photograph at left was taken in 1911, the year the E.A. Minor Masonic Lodge was founded and began meeting there. Below, the seventh-grade class at East Atlanta School took their class picture in 1908 on the front steps of the new building. (Both courtesy of Martha Brown United Methodist Church.)

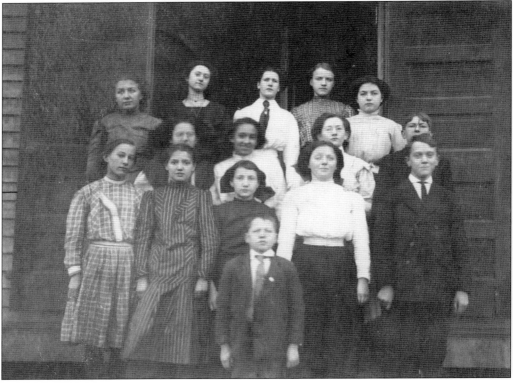

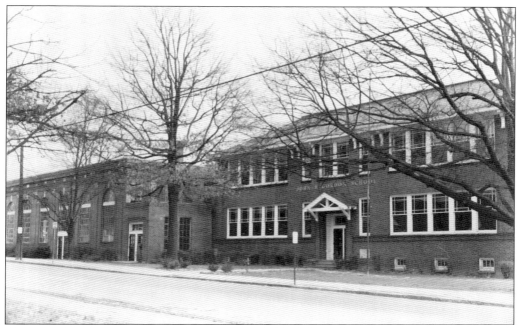

After being annexed by Atlanta in 1909, there was a push to construct a larger and more modern school for the growing number of children. The new East Atlanta School was completed by 1915 on Metropolitan Avenue at a cost of about $15,000. It featured eight large classrooms, a principal's office, teachers' restrooms, a library, and student restrooms. The school is seen above in the 1950s with additions. The young class below, in 1917, was among the first to start the tradition of taking class pictures on the front steps of the school building. (Above, courtesy of the Wagnon family; below, courtesy of Donald Stephen Clarke.)

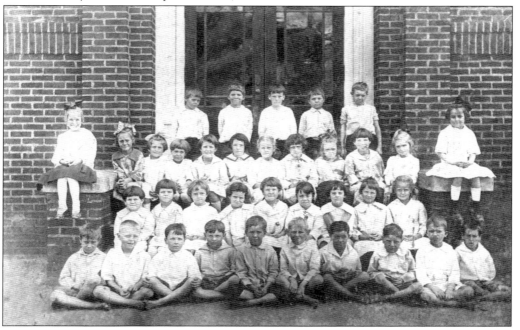

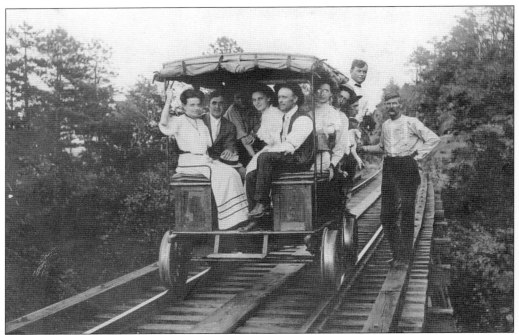

Stone Mountain was a popular destination for a picnic. This group of East Atlanta friends traveled there for an outing in a handcar, possibly along the Georgia Railroad (now CSX) tracks. (Courtesy of Mary Frances Banks.)

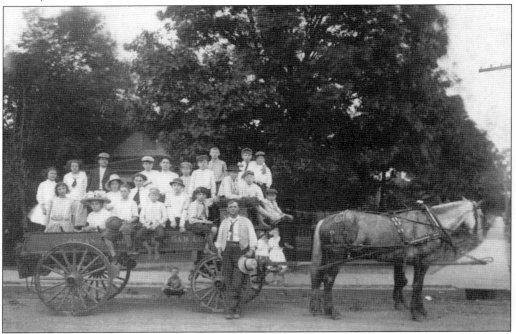

Members of the Marbut & Minor families piled into a wagon for a picnic around 1900. This photograph was probably taken at the corner of Flat Shoals and Metropolitan Avenues. (Courtesy of the Everitt family.)

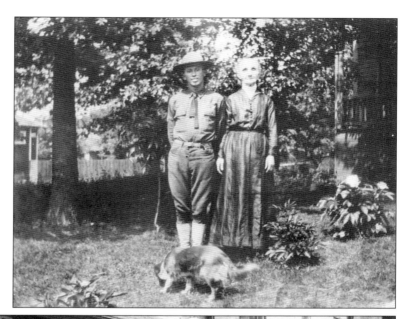

James White prepared to go overseas in 1918 when the United States entered World War I. He visited with his aunt Martha White Clarke at her home on Sanders Avenue while still in training. Clarke was the daughter of Benjamin Franklin White, compiler of the shape note songbook *The Sacred Harp*. (Courtesy of Donald Stephen Clarke.)

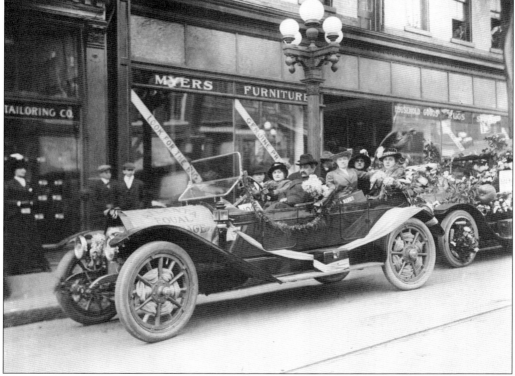

Moreland Avenue residents Margaret (back seat, center) and Katherine (back seat, right) Koch participated in a suffrage float in a 1913 Atlanta civic parade. Katherine served as president of the Georgia Woman Suffrage Association from 1901 to 1904. The 19th Amendment, ratified on August 18, 1920, gave women the right to vote, but Georgia women could not vote until the 1922 elections. (Courtesy of Kenan Research Center at the Atlanta History Center.)

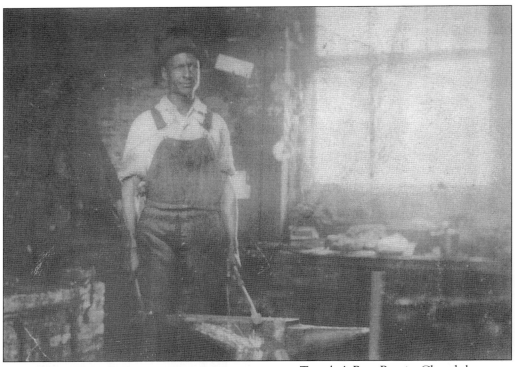

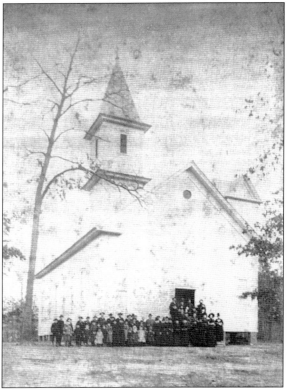

Traveler's Rest Baptist Church began as an African American Sunday school and prayer-meeting group in a former rest stop on Flat Shoals Avenue. Wheat Street Baptist Church organized it as Traveler's Rest Baptist Church in 1876, with Rev. Martin Scruggs (above) as pastor. Several East Atlanta businessmen purchased the property in the 1920s. The church relocated and continues today. The cemetery was moved in the 1930s. (Courtesy of Greater Traveler's Rest Baptist Church.)

In 1873, Mary Jane Terry agreed to sell one acre of land to the Methodist Episcopal Church South if the church would name the meeting place after her recently deceased son, Sylvester. Their one-story building was called Sylvester Meeting House. The Missionary Baptist Church purchased the property and built this larger two-story structure in 1887 across the street, naming it Sylvester Baptist Church. (Courtesy of Mary Frances Banks.)

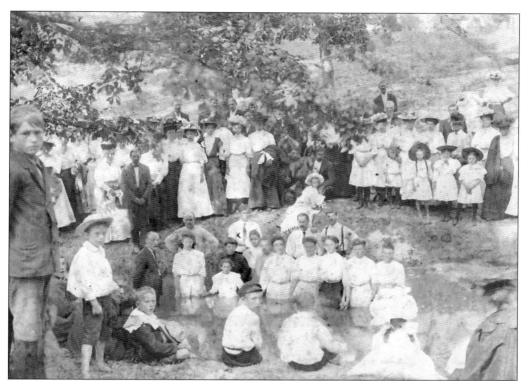

Above, members of Sylvester Baptist Church gathered off-site at a small pond near Confederate Avenue for a baptism service in 1908. The church was located near Clifton Road and Flat Shoals Road. (Courtesy of Sandra Moody.)

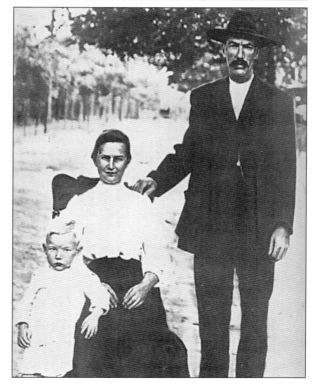

J.W. McWilliams purchased about seven acres of land near Sylvester Church from Mary Jane Terry in 1876 to be used as a public cemetery. It quickly became known as Sylvester Cemetery. Marcus Hasty, standing here with his wife, Mary "Ohmie" Hasty, and grandson Mark Wilson, was the caretaker of Sylvester Cemetery when this photograph was taken in 1910. (Courtesy of Martha Brown United Methodist Church.)

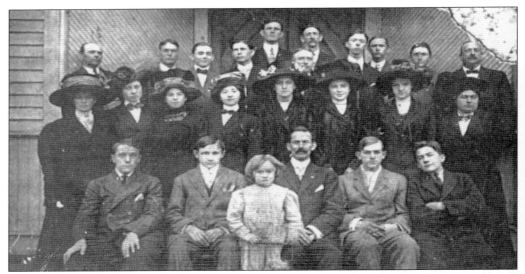

The East Atlanta Methodist Church first met as the Union Sunday school in the home of Mark Minor on Flat Shoals Avenue in 1892, and then in this frame building, constructed at the corner of Granberry (now Metropolitan Place) and Metropolitan Avenues in 1897 or 1898. Professor S.A. Merchant's Sunday school class posed for this photograph on the day after Christmas in 1911. (Courtesy of Mary Frances Banks.)

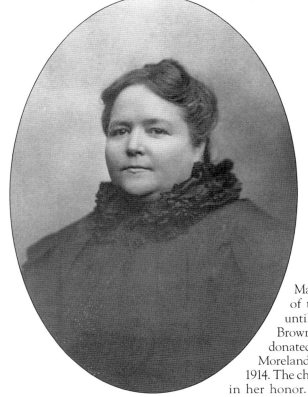

Martha Stewart Brown was an active member of the East Atlanta Methodist Church until she died in 1907. Her husband, John F. Brown, a son of James "Spanish Jim" Brown, donated land at the corner of Metropolitan and Moreland Avenues for a new church building in 1914. The church was completed in 1918 and renamed in her honor. (Courtesy of Mary Frances Banks.)

Three

THRIVING AND SURVIVING

By the 1920s, East Atlanta boasted of being the place where "homes are happy and business good." Now established as an independent community within Atlanta, it offered the advantages of numerous churches, civic associations, and schools. The fast-growing area was served by John B. Gordon Elementary School, John F. Faith Elementary School (which also served as the Atlanta Normal Teacher School), and Bouldercrest Elementary School, in rural DeKalb County. The commercial district attracted dozens of new businesses that drew in the surrounding communities. The opening of the classy Madison Theatre in 1927 made East Atlanta's main street a destination for families and children throughout the week. Grocery stores remained open on Saturdays until midnight so that farmers and dairymen and their families who came into town had time to shop, catch a first-run movie, and return to pick up their groceries by store closing. In 1928, the community celebrated 30 years of progress and the arrival of streetlights in the business district with a street gala that included dancing on the newly paved Flat Shoals and Glenwood Avenues.

Times were tight during the Depression years, but the community remained strong. Relying on one another like a large extended family, some businesses extended credit when possible, telling customers to pay when they could. Many East Atlanta teenagers helped out by working at Piggly Wiggly, located in the old Marbut & Minor building, or at the A&P, two doors down from the Madison Theatre, making as much as $2.50 a week. Delivery boys and soda jerks at East Atlanta Pharmacy and Archer's Drug Store could make 10¢ an hour.

Even though the community struggled, the future held promise, with churches and schools bursting at their seams. While some businesses marked time and some families lost their homes, the paving of Moreland Avenue past Ormewood Avenue in 1932 was a sign of better days to come for future residential and commercial development. East Atlanta dug in its heels and grew.

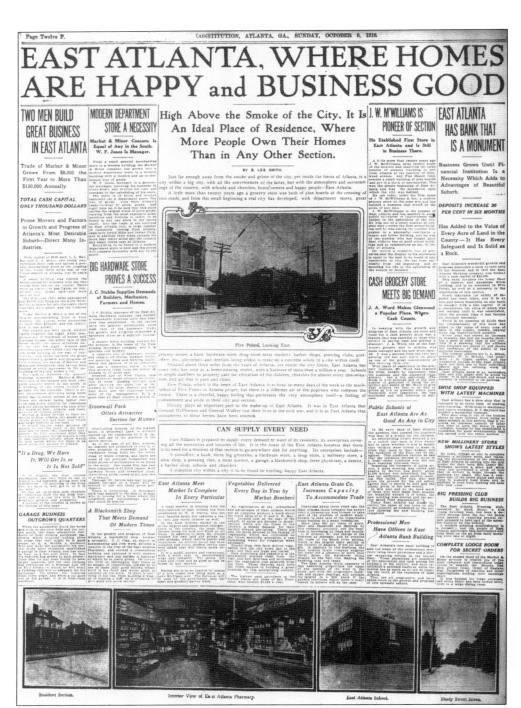

This October 8, 1916, promotional page in the *Atlanta Constitution* expresses the suburban optimism and growth of the once-rural community. Boasting of its clean air, pure water, pastoral landscape, and modern conveniences, business leaders and developers were eager to attract a group of hardworking people with dreams of owning their own homes or businesses. (Courtesy of Katina VanCronkhite.)

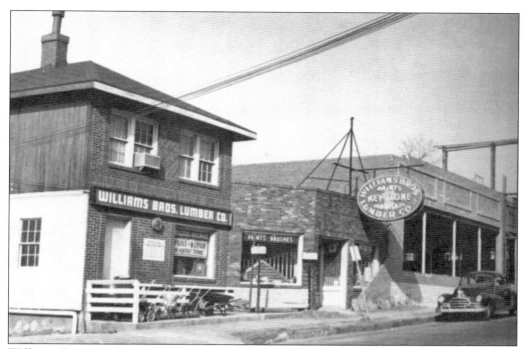

Williams Bros. Lumber Company opened its doors in 1922 on Glenwood Avenue with four employees, a wagon, and two mules named Big Boy and Old Joe. Members of the Williams family moved to East Atlanta in the 1920s and founded several other successful construction and real estate businesses. The lumber company provided building materials and millwork for the booming housing industry after World War II. As Atlanta grew with expressways and skyscrapers, the business reached across Georgia. By the 1960s, the family had developed their acreage in East Atlanta, consolidating and expanding their operations on land south of the new Interstate 20 (below) to include their office headquarters; a manufacturing and distribution center; and paint, concrete, and sand facilities. The business continued through the 1990s. The Williams family, through their various businesses, became eminent leaders and philanthropists in Georgia. (Both courtesy of the Williams family.)

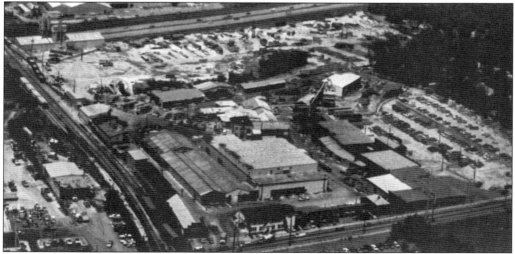

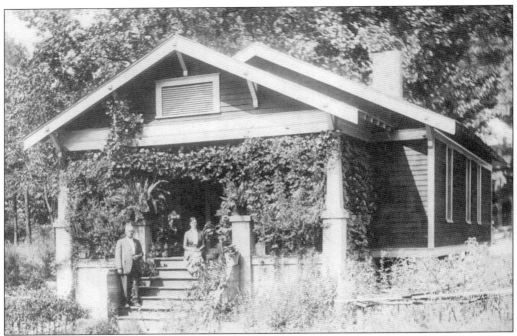

Amos Van Epps migrated to the South from New York, settling in Atlanta after the Civil War. After his death, his widow, Julia, subdivided a portion of his 101-plus-acre farm in 1912 for a residential development off of Flat Shoals Avenue. Van Vleck Avenue was named for his mother's family. Through the 1930s, the Van Epps family traveled East Atlanta's byways in their distinctive electric car. Above, Tom Lindsey Sr. and his wife, Mamie, were among the first to live in the subdivision, at 1408 Van Epps Avenue, in 1917. Below, the Mathews family lived nearby, at 1419 Van Epps, for 40 years. H.T. Mathews was a linotype operator at the *Atlanta Constitution* and, later, a lawyer. His wife, Betty Lou, and daughter Joyce are seen here dressed for an Easter church service. (Above, courtesy of Tom Lindsey Jr.; below, courtesy of the Pattillo family.)

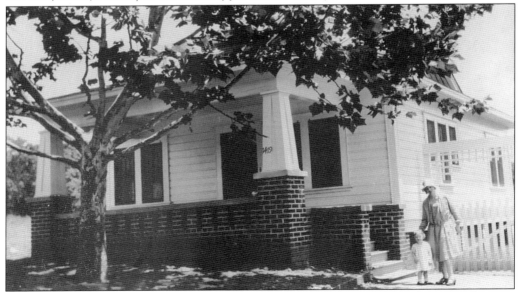

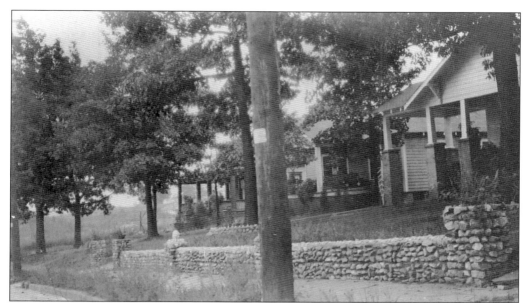

James and Odessa Puckett bought their home at 1439 Metropolitan Avenue (above) in 1928 and built the fence out of stones found on the property. James Puckett survived an electrocution working the wires for the Postal Telegraph Company in Tennessee and later opened the Yum Yum Café on Flat Shoals Avenue in the 1930s. (Courtesy of the Puckett family.)

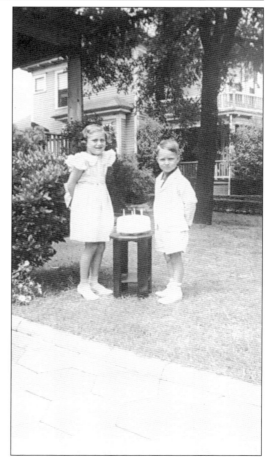

The Wagnon family had an annual tradition of taking a photograph of birthday boy Charles Wagnon with his cake on the front lawn of their home on Metropolitan Avenue. Here, he celebrates a birthday around 1935 with his aunt Marylyn Matchette. The house seen in the background was owned by the family of East Atlanta butcher William Bartow Owens. (Courtesy of the Wagnon family.)

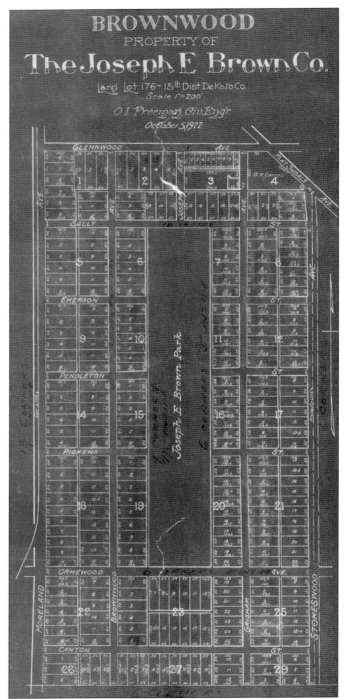

The Brownwood Park subdivision began development in 1922. It was laid out so that the small lots for homes had ready access to the 13-acre green space donated by the Joseph E. Brown family. Note the Confederate Soldiers' Home streetcar line running along Moreland Avenue and turning off at Ormewood Avenue. (Courtesy of Henry Bryant.)

Georgia's Civil War governor, Joseph E. Brown, acquired the western half of Land Lot 177 in East Atlanta, which had once been the plantation of James Calhoun, the mayor of Atlanta during the war. Brown also served in the US senate from 1880 to 1890. His son Julius developed the land after his death. (Courtesy of the Library of Congress.)

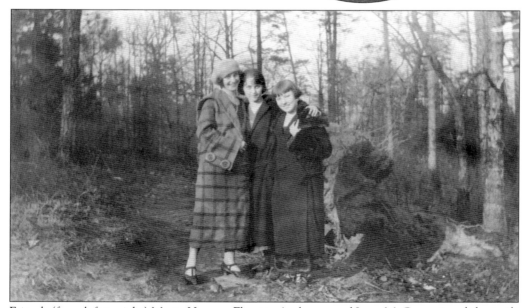

Friends (from left to right) Myrta Haynes, Floretta Ambrose, and Lucy McGee enjoyed the trails of Joseph E. Brown Park even on this chilly day in 1924. The original park deed required that half of the land remain in its natural, undeveloped state. (Courtesy of Donald Stephen Clarke.)

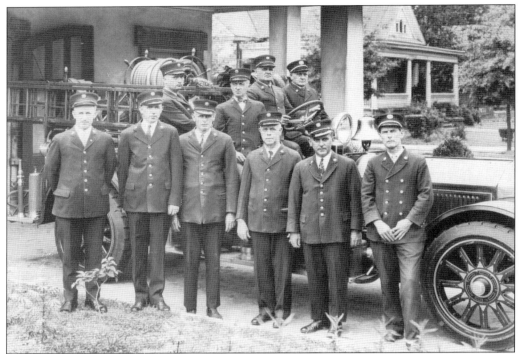

Fire Station No. 13 opened in 1921 on the corner of Flat Shoals and Metropolitan Avenues. Charles B. Everitt's original home is in the background, where a new fire station was built in 2008. Lt. Col. William Jones, the owner of an Indiana store where a young Abraham Lincoln once clerked, was killed on this site during the Battle of Atlanta. (Courtesy of Kenan Research Center at the Atlanta History Center.)

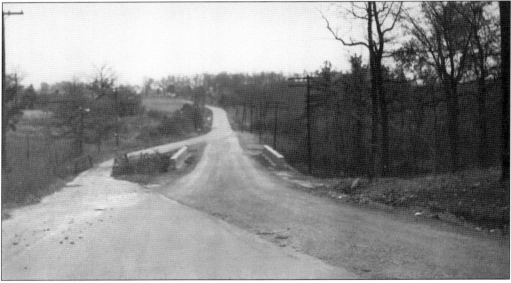

Road improvements became a necessity as the area was developed and highway travel increased. In 1928, the county built a new bridge with granite arches over Sugar Creek on Flat Shoals Avenue, near Fayetteville Road, at a cost of $6,491. (Courtesy of the DeKalb County Public Library.)

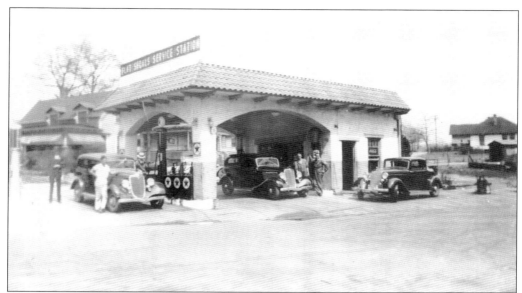

Elijah S. Clarke, whose car is on the far right, took the photograph above of customers filling up with Texaco gas at the Flat Shoals Service Station, on the corner of May Avenue, in 1934. Clarke's grandfather was an early settler in East Atlanta. (Courtesy of Donald Stephen Clarke.)

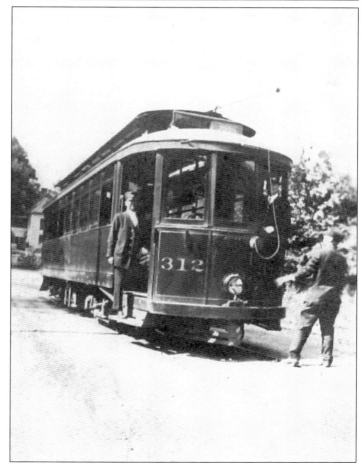

George Turner, standing on the streetcar, moved to the East Atlanta area around 1914 and became a conductor on the Confederate Soldiers' Home line. It cost 5¢ for children and 10¢ for adults to ride the streetcar throughout the city and beyond, with transfers, when this photograph was taken in the 1930s. (Courtesy of Katherine Carter.)

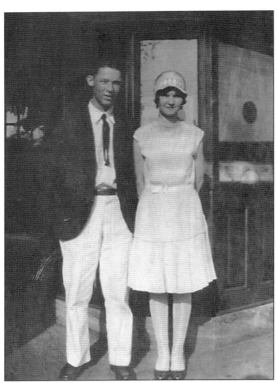

It was a day out on the town in 1927 for W.L. Wagnon and his date, Louise Graham. At left, they are standing in front of the newly opened Madison Theatre. Below, Wagnon's brother-in-law Tom West (left) and sister Frances Wagnon West (second from left) joined the pair for a photograph in front of the East Atlanta Bank. (Both courtesy of the Wagnon family.)

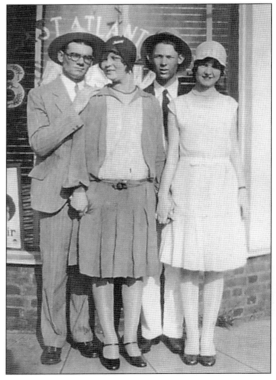

The Madison Theatre opened on July 2, 1927, on Flat Shoals Avenue. According to this advertisement in the *Atlanta Constitution*, it cost over $85,000 to build. Designed in the popular Moorish Revival style, it seated over 600 and had a $5,000 pipe organ that provided musical accompaniment to the silent films. By 1934, the organ had become obsolete and was purchased for Martha Brown United Methodist Church. (Courtesy of Katina VanCronkhite.)

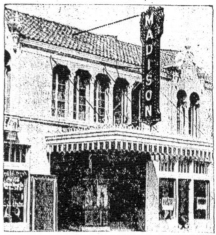

The New
MADISON THEATRE
496 Flat Shoals Ave., S. E.

DANIELL & BEUTELL, ARCHITECTS

Open Today, July 2nd
AT 1:15 P. M.

All East Atlanta, Atlanta and the south is proud of the splendid new Madison Theater, which opens today. It surpasses any community theater in the city or state and is equaled in magnificence and splendor by no other save one in the entire south. Throughout, it is splendidly constructed and appointed; and the ventilating and seating arrangements assure patrons the utmost comfort. The cost of the theater amounted to much over $85,000.

Miss Evelyn Clair, Universal screen star and favorite, will attend the opening celebration.

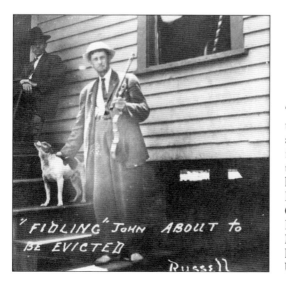

"Fiddlin' John" Carson, the first musician to broadcast old-time country music, attended Sylvester Church and is buried in its cemetery. In 1923, Carson launched the country music–recording industry with his phonograph record for the Okeh label. He faced eviction in 1914 from his nearby Cabbagetown residence during the Fulton Bag & Cotton Mills strike. (Photograph by Mrs. E.B. Smith, George Meany Memorial Labor Archives, courtesy of Georgia State University's Southern Labor Archives.)

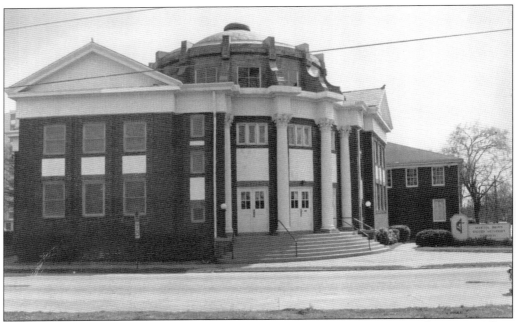

Martha Brown Memorial Methodist Church was completed in 1918 in the popular Dayton Plan, with four colossal Corinthian columns and a domed auditorium. The building was one of seven in Atlanta honored by the Urban Commission on Outstanding Design in 1956. In 1987, the Atlanta Urban Design Commission placed it in its inventory of significant historic properties. Below, members gathered in 1928 for the dedication of the new educational building, seen on the right. By that time, membership had grown to over 1,500. (Both courtesy of Martha Brown United Methodist Church.)

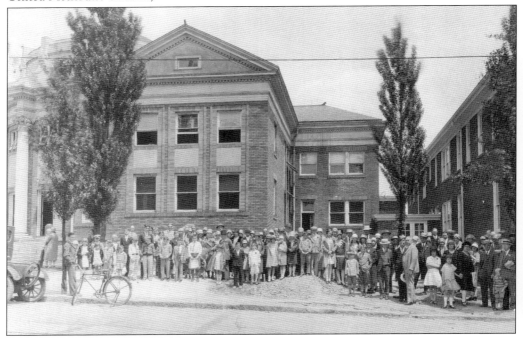

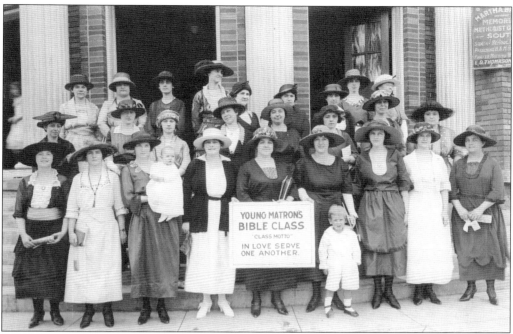

Martha Brown United Methodist Church was a center for spiritual, social, and community activities in East Atlanta throughout the 1920s and 1930s. Following its motto, "In Love Serve One Another," the 1925 Young Matrons Class included many prominent women in the community. The children were equally involved in church and community activities. Below, in 1933, they participate in a Tom Thumb wedding, which was a popular fundraising play. (Both courtesy of Martha Brown United Methodist Church.)

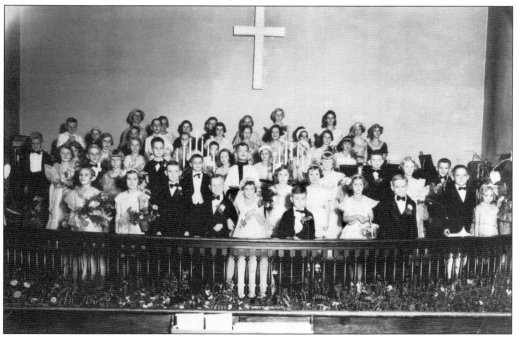

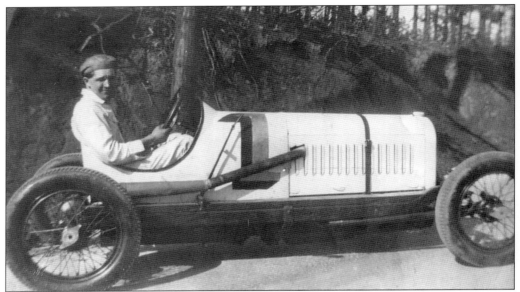

Wesley Argoe built the race car above in the late 1920s or early 1930s and test drove it on Flat Shoals Avenue. Seen below with driver Buddy Calloway in 1932, Argoe, converted an aircraft engine to power this race car, which was called the fastest racing machine in the South. It was believed to be the first car from the Deep South taken to race at the Indianapolis Motor Speedway. Unfortunately, the vehicle failed the technical inspection there and was disqualified. (Above, courtesy of the Argoe family; below, courtesy of Indianapolis Motor Speedway.)

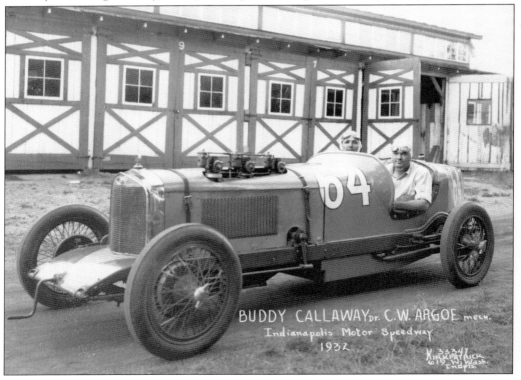

Charlie Everitt grew up in East Atlanta and founded his own grocery store (right) at the southwest corner of Flat Shoals and Glenwood Avenues. Residents regularly called to order the freshest groceries for delivery to their homes. Everitt helped carry the neighborhood through the Depression with his generous credit policies. A silent-movie theater was reportedly located in the left side of the building seen below in 1938, near Flat Shoals and Stokeswood Avenues. The Atlantic Company sold coal and ice on the right side. The left side later became a bowling alley, employing local youths as pinsetters for 2¢ or 3¢ per game. Other youths broke in their new roller skates at Christmas on the pavement between the icehouse and the bridge at Sugar Creek. (Right, courtesy of the Everitt family; below, courtesy of the Wagnon family.)

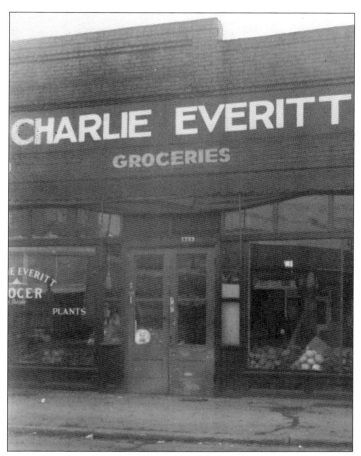

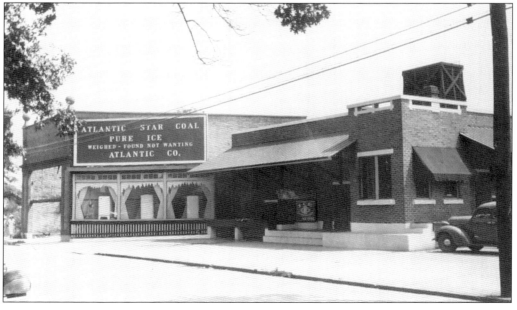

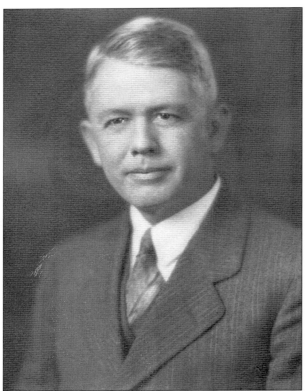

Joseph Charlie "J.C." Murphy was a prominent East Atlanta community leader and an alderman, school board member, and city attorney in the city of Atlanta. He and his family built a home at the corner of Metropolitan and Patterson Avenues in 1920. J.C. Murphy Junior High School, which later became J.C. Murphy High School, was named in his honor. (Courtesy of the Murphy family.)

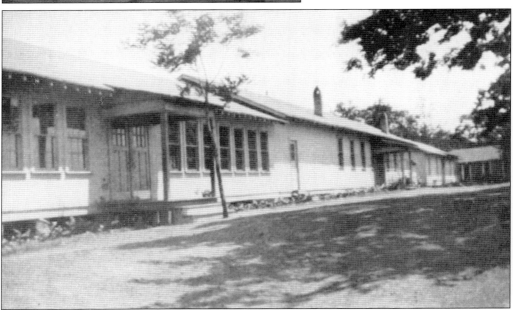

J.C. Murphy was an advocate for public education in East Atlanta and lobbied for a local junior high school. To make the goal financially feasible, World War I barracks at Camp Gordon (now Peachtree DeKalb Airport) were moved to a plateau on Memorial Drive (today's Walker Park) and utilized as portable classrooms. (Courtesy of the Atlanta Independent School System.)

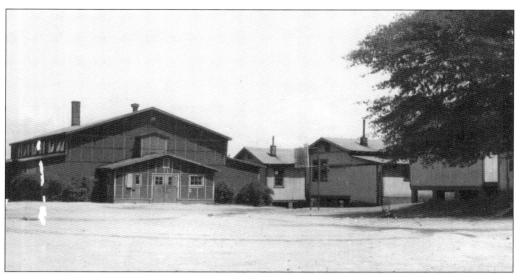

The gymnasium above was added to the old barracks classroom buildings at J.C. Murphy Junior High School, which were heated by potbellied stoves. At right, Katherine Turner (left) celebrates her graduation day with friends Malissa Scheltert (center) and June Lewis (right) in 1933. The girls were required to wear matching dresses of exactly the same hem length. Upon graduation, girls would continue their studies at Girls High School in Grant Park and boys would attend either Boys High School or Tech High School in midtown. (Both courtesy of Katherine Carter.)

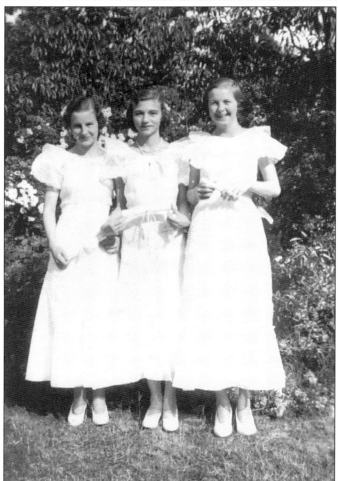

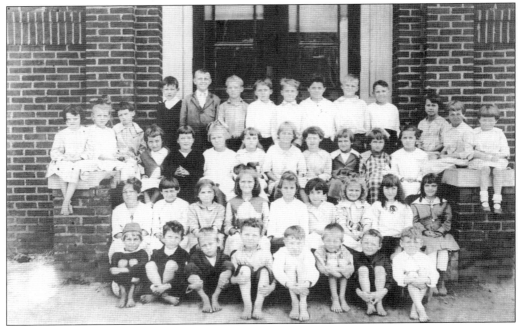

Many children enjoyed attending East Atlanta School barefoot during the warmer months. The first-grade students above sit for their class picture in 1920 on the front steps of the new school building, completed in 1915. The school was renamed John B. Gordon School in 1923, the year the seventh-graders below graduated. (Above, courtesy of David Floyd; below, courtesy of Martha Brown United Methodist Church.)

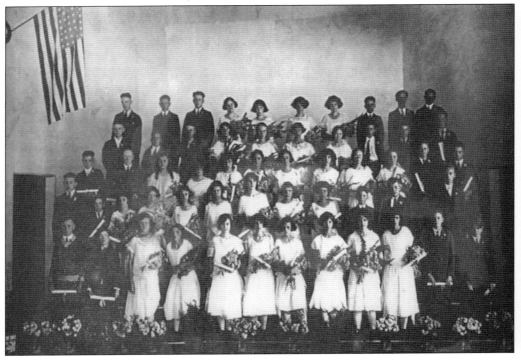

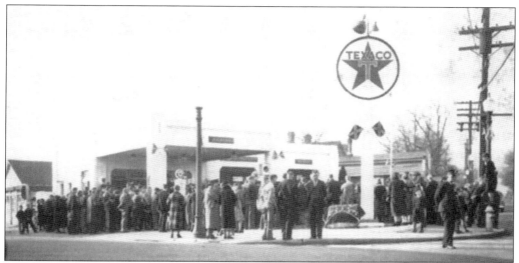

The E.A. Minor Lodge instigated many community improvements and activities. In 1938, they funded a monument at the corner of Flat Shoals and Glenwood Avenues, seen above by the Texaco sign. Gov. E.D. Rivers and Atlanta mayor William B. Hartsfield attended the dedication. The bronze plaque noted that the Smith-Gresham division of the 17th Corps held this pivotal front-line position during the Battle of Atlanta. Below, East Atlanta Chapter No. 108 of the Order of the Eastern Star inducts a new worthy matron. The formal ceremony was held at the E.A. Minor Masonic Lodge hall, on the second floor of the Piggly Wiggly grocery store, which stood on the site of the former Marbut & Minor grocery store. (Above, courtesy of the Everitt family; below, courtesy of the Wagnon family.)

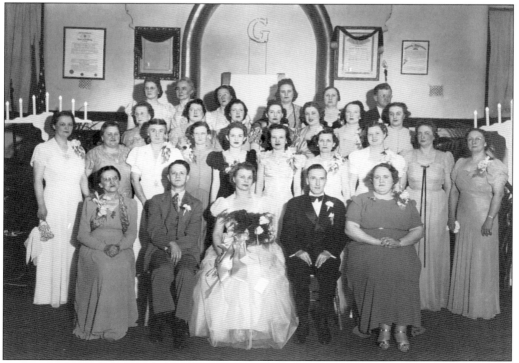

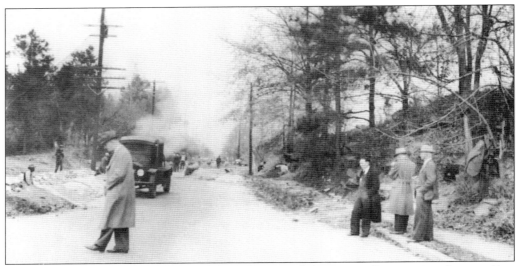

In 1925, Moreland Avenue was paved from Ormewood Avenue to Constitution Avenue. East Atlanta resident and councilman George B. Lyle (left foreground), the chairman of the city's streets committee, arranged for the public works project to be completed. Children were often let out of school to greet Pres. Franklin Roosevelt, who frequently traveled this "New Macon Highway" to his Warm Springs retreat. (Courtesy of the Connie and Scott Lyle Callaway family.)

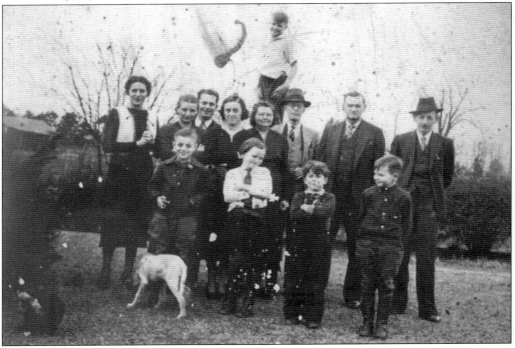

To the south of East Atlanta along Bouldercrest Drive and Flat Shoals Avenue were many small farms and dairies. The extended Floyd family brought in the new year of 1938 at their family home on Bouldercrest Drive. The children, including David Floyd (first row, left) and Mary Ann Floyd Hightower (first row, center), were dressed for a ride on Mary Ann's pony. (Courtesy of David Floyd.)

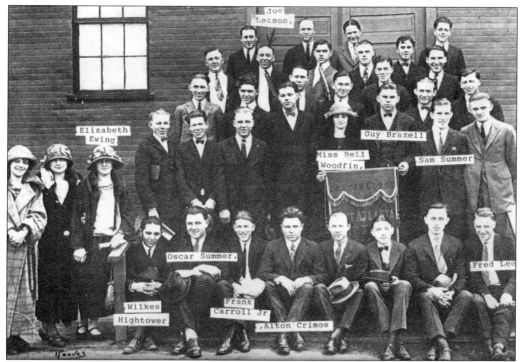

In 1902, Gov. Joseph E. Brown deeded property to the East Atlanta Baptist Church at Glenwood and Joseph Avenues for $1. Brown had been a longtime Baptist deacon and teacher, his father-in-law was a minister, and his wife was a church stalwart. Above, one of the Sunday school classes, the Berean Class, gathered in 1924, probably on the steps of the original building. The East Atlanta Baptist Church was renamed Moreland Avenue Baptist Church when it acquired a new site (below) on Moreland Avenue in 1922. (Above, courtesy of Martha Brown United Methodist Church; below, courtesy of the Atlanta Independent School System.)

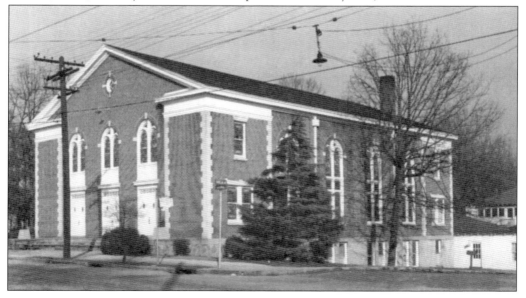

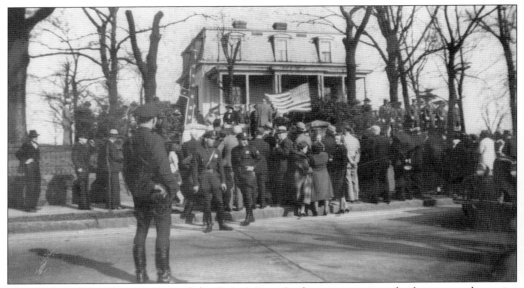

The Order of the Eastern Star of the E.A. Minor Lodge commissioned a bronze-and-granite monument for the front lawn of the Koch house, at 232 Moreland Avenue. The monument commemorated the bloody Civil War battle fought on Leggett's Hill. This location is now the westbound half of the Interstate 20 cloverleaf at Moreland Avenue. (Courtesy of Kenan Research Center at the Atlanta History Center.)

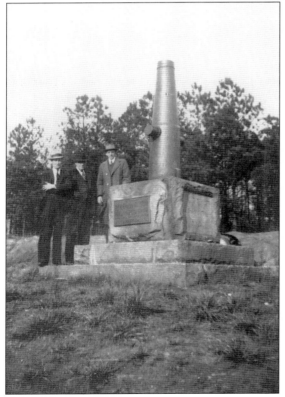

In 1938, the Walker Monument was moved to its correct location, on the eastern side of Sugar Creek on Glenwood Avenue. The location's authenticity was verified by historian Franklin Garrett (left), standing with Beverly DuBose Sr. (center) and Fay Robarts (right). The small triangle of land outside of the city limits was donated by the Ashford and Hunnicutt estates for an Atlanta park. The adjacent property was becoming the Parkview subdivision. (Courtesy of Kenan Research Center at the Atlanta History Center.)

Four

WORLD WAR II AND THE BOOM

When World War II erupted, East Atlanta was a small, close-knit community where residents could still greet most people on the street by their first name. Though neighbors tried to keep life as normal as possible, the war brought substantial changes to the area. Strict gas and food rationing made the war abroad very real at home. Many young men left to fight across the world, while others at home carpooled across town to Marietta for jobs at the Bell Bomber plant. Women stepped up to take over positions—such as streetcar conductor—left vacant by departing soldiers. Organizations like the Martha Brown Friendly Bible Class gathered to make surgical bandages for the Red Cross.

The children did their part, too. Students from Gordon Elementary School occasionally sang patriotic songs at neighborhood homes, which displayed either a blue star for each family member serving in the military or a gold star for a family member killed. Young Marion Blackwell, hearing the sound of a sputtering aircraft engine near his home on Bouldercrest Drive, rushed toward the crash site to help. He was the first to discover the Naval Air Station Atlanta pilot wrapped in his parachute and emerging safely from a ravine near Carroll's Lake, now called Glen Emerald Lake.

The end of the war signaled a new boom. There were 15,000 residents in East Atlanta by the end of the 1940s, and more than 500 new homes were built within a block of the bank. The neighborhood also got a new library in 1949, and Atlanta stores like Jacob's Drugs and Sunshine Department Store established suburban locations in East Atlanta. Locally owned businesses such as E.V. Harris Printing and Floyd Brothers provided local jobs and enhanced East Atlanta's reputation. Growth continued through the 1950s, expanding the residential neighborhood eastward from the commercial district and necessitating the building of the new East Atlanta High School, which opened in 1958 to relieve overcrowding. East Atlanta was booming, its reputation was growing, and residents were proud to call it home.

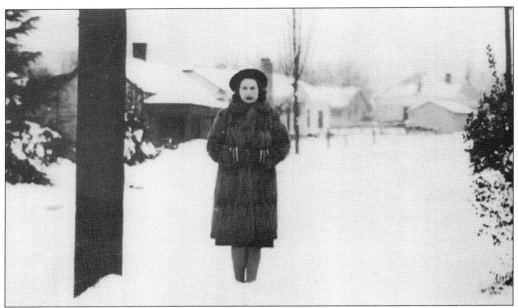

Atlanta was covered with a record snowfall in January 1940. Pauline Knox bundled up in her fur coat near her home at 465 Haas Avenue, with Metropolitan Place in the background. The East Atlanta post office replaced the three homes and buildings at the far end of the street in 1962. (Courtesy of E.C. Knox.)

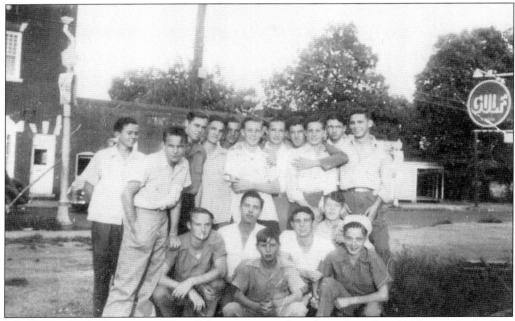

The Rinky-Dinks, a group of East Atlanta teenage friends, gathered in 1940 outside the East Atlanta Pharmacy, where Charles "Buck" Pattillo (standing, fifth from right) was a soda jerk and delivery boy. By 1942, all the Rinky-Dinks but the youngest were fighting in World War II. Buddy Waits (kneeling, left), a gunner on a B-17 that was shot down, was the only one killed in the war. (Courtesy of Charles "Buck" Pattillo.)

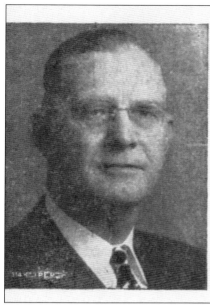

East Atlantan George Lyle was a popular Atlanta City Council member. In May 1942, he served briefly as the mayor of Atlanta when Mayor Roy LeCraw resigned to join the Army after defeating incumbent William Hartsfield. Lyle, as mayor pro tem, held the office until new elections could be held. (Courtesy of the Connie and Scott Lyle Callaway family.)

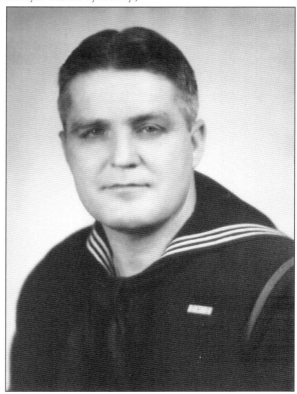

Living on Hemlock Avenue with his wife and three children, Herbert Tolar, though exempt from the draft, was first in line at the Atlanta Navy recruiting office on December 8, 1941, the day after the bombing of Pearl Harbor. He served until the end of the war and was awarded the Silver Star. (Courtesy of Mary Frances Banks.)

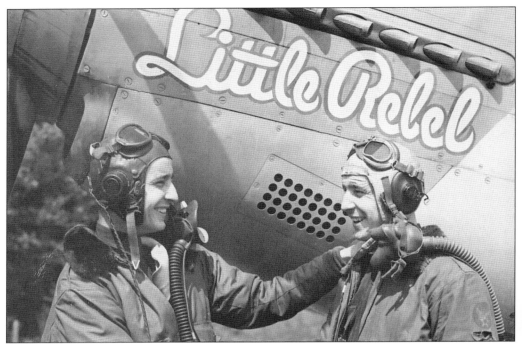

Twins Charles "Buck" and Cuthbert "Bill" Pattillo grew up on Metropolitan Avenue. They enlisted in the Army Air Corps when they graduated high school in 1942 and became decorated combat pilots during World War II. They went on to have distinguished military careers. Bill retired as a major general and Buck retired as a lieutenant general. (Courtesy of Sam Sox Jr., Photography Archivist, 352nd Fighter Group Association.)

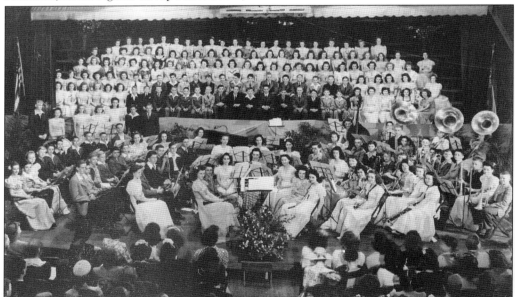

Some aspects of home and school life went uninterrupted in the early years of the war. The 1942 Murphy Junior High School orchestra gave a concert for parents and students in the gymnasium, which featured a stage. (Courtesy of David Floyd.)

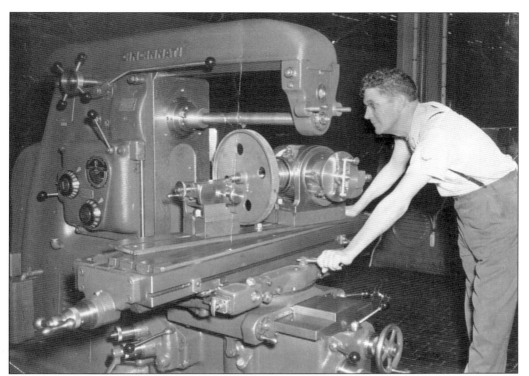

Mechanic and race-car driver Wesley Argoe (above) worked in the Bell Bomber B-29 assembly plant that opened in Marietta in 1942. He drove a carpool for neighborhood "Rosie the Riveters," joining 40,000 others in the Atlanta area who utilized their skills for the war effort. (Courtesy of the Argoe family.)

W.L. Wagnon completed training to become an air raid warden, as indicated by his certificate from the Atlanta Municipal Defense Council. Air raid wardens trained for 25 hours to learn first aid, fire- and gas-defense procedures, and blackout-drill supervision. They received a billy club and an armband and were to set an "example of cool efficiency under all conditions." (Courtesy of the Wagnon family.)

Certificate of Instructions

This is to certify that

W. L. WAGNON,

has satisfactorily completed the Required Courses of Training and demonstrated the necessary knowledge and ability to carry out the duties thereof and is entitled to wear the Official Emblem of the Citizens Defense Corps and the insignia designated him

AIR RAID WARDEN

of the Atlanta Municipal Defense Council

Room 206, City Hall,
Atlanta, Georgia,
May 5, 1942.

COMMANDER

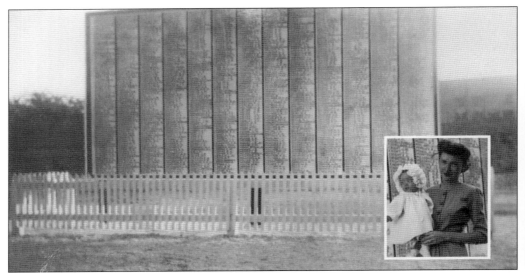

This wooden memorial was erected on Flat Shoals Avenue to honor all the neighborhood men and women killed in World War II. In the inset on the right, Lucille "Tootsie" Lyle Calloway (later Lucille "Tootsie" Lyle Elkins), the daughter of city councilman George Lyle, holds her daughter Connie in front of the memorial, which was removed before 1949 to make way for the new library. (Courtesy of Martha Brown United Methodist Church; inset, courtesy of the Connie and Scott Lyle Callaway family.)

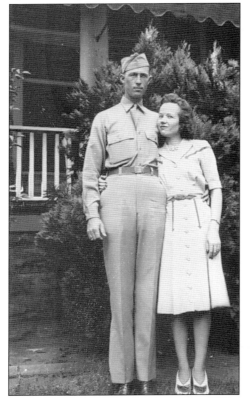

Finding housing was often a challenge in the 1940s. Frank and Celeste "Smitty" Jones lived in the four upstairs rooms of the Wagnon home on Metropolitan Avenue during the war years. When Frank returned after the war, he and Smitty moved into their own home in Brownwood Park. (Courtesy of the Wagnon family.)

Grace Bradshaw operated Bradshaw's Café from around 1944 to 1950 on Flat Shoals Avenue. The price adjustments on her menu below reflect rising food costs after the war. At right, Martha Gautier sits underneath the sign to Bradshaw's on a sign advertising another popular hangout, Harry's Sandwich Shop and Pool Room, located on Glenwood Avenue. (Courtesy of Martha Brown United Methodist Church.)

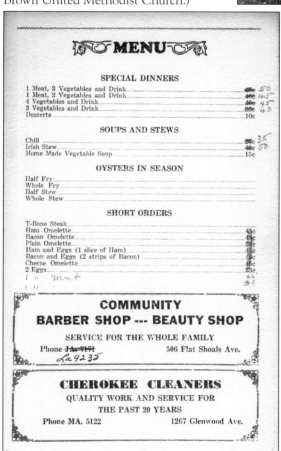

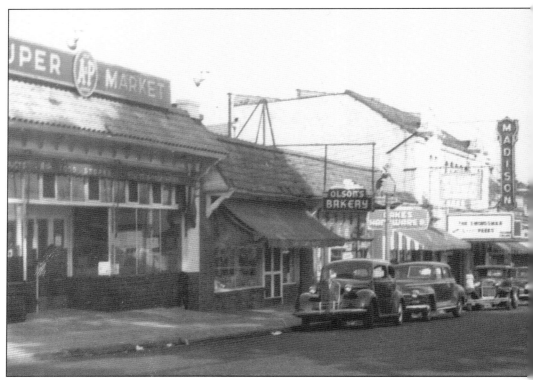

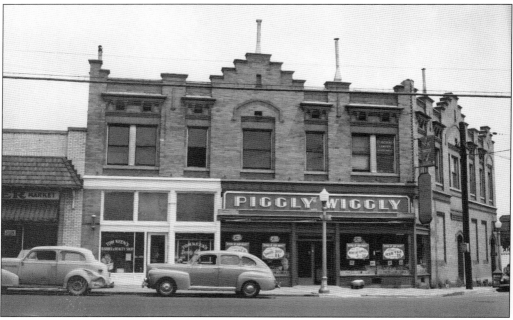

This building, on the site of the former Marbut & Minor store, was built by 1933 to accommodate the growing E.A. Minor Lodge, which met upstairs, and the neighborhood's first Piggly Wiggly self-service grocery store, on the first floor. (Courtesy of Georgia State University Special Collections and Archives.)

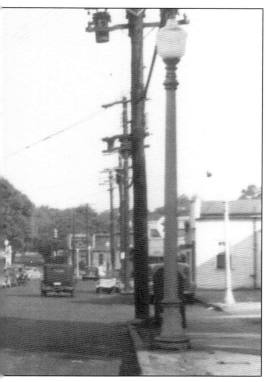

The East Atlanta Business District, along Flat Shoals Avenue, was growing and prospering throughout the 1940s. In 1949, when this photograph was taken, 10 new businesses had opened within one block of the East Atlanta Bank. Among the thriving enterprises in East Atlanta were seven grocery stores, seven restaurants, five beauty parlors or barbershops, three hardware stores, three farm-supply stores, and a newspaper. (Courtesy of Louis Arnold.)

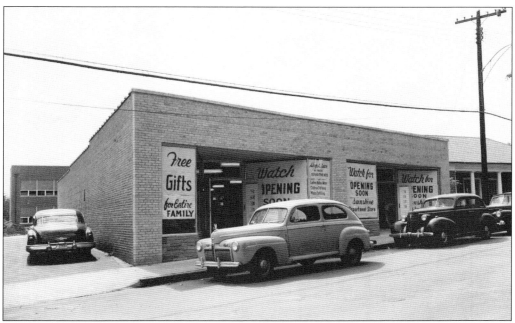

Sunshine Department Store expanded from its popular downtown discount store to its first suburban location, next to the library on Flat Shoals Avenue, in 1951. The Sunshine family later moved the store to Sunshine Plaza, south of East Atlanta on Moreland Avenue. (Courtesy of Georgia State University Special Collections and Archives.)

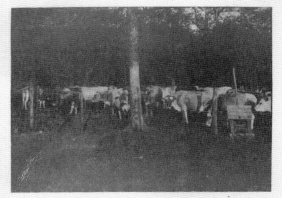

Dairies dotted the land surrounding East Atlanta from its early days. Charles O. Smith called his cows "the best herd of cows in the county" in this 1912 advertisement. In 1943, his son Samuel E. Smith and Hiram Stubbs founded Atlanta Dairies, a cooperative of small dairy farms that built a pasteurization plant on Memorial Drive after Georgia passed a costly compulsory-pasteurization law. (Courtesy of the DeKalb History Center.)

By the 1930s, DeKalb County had more dairies than any county outside the state of Wisconsin. James Frank Gazaway and his son Frank Marion operated Gazaway & Son Dairy on the edge of East Atlanta. Below, around 1940, James watches his three-year-old daughter Evelyn experience her first horse ride in front of the family home. The dairy relocated to Clifton Springs and remained active until 1957. (Courtesy of Claudia Gazaway Stucke.)

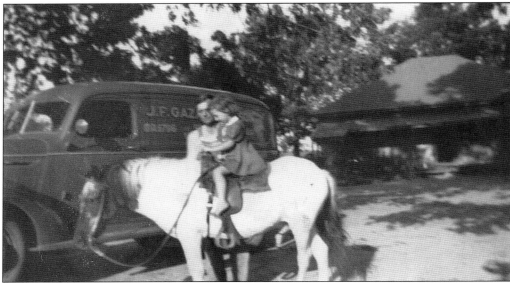

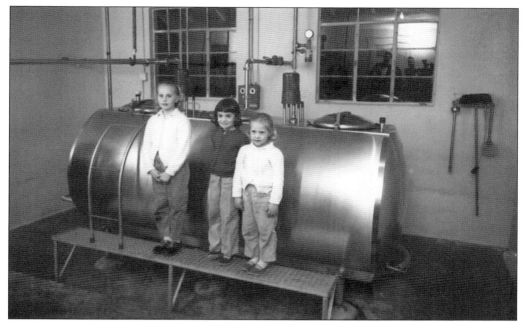

Standing from left to right, Winn, Lynn, and Sheryl Smith show off the first milk cooler installed at the Smith dairy farm around 1959. Milk from the cows in the adjoining room was piped into the cooler tank and kept cold until it could be transported. Before this, milk cans were submerged in a concrete pool filled with cool well water. (Courtesy of Winn S. Floyd.)

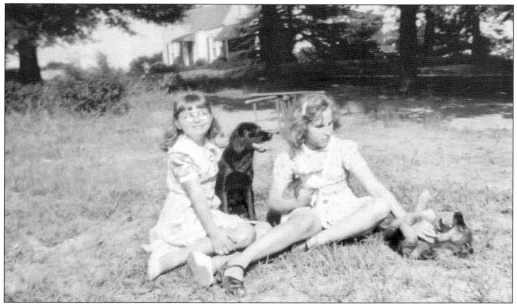

W.C. Gill founded the 83-acre Oakgrove Dairy on Moreland Avenue in the late 1800s. After the Depression, the family sold everything but their home to their manager, Cliff Knuckles, and it became Knuckles Dairy. Here, Catherine Perry (right), Gill's great-granddaughter, plays with the family dogs near the Knuckles and Perry homes with friend Betty Whatley. The property was sold in 2000 to make way for a shopping center. (Courtesy of the Perry family.)

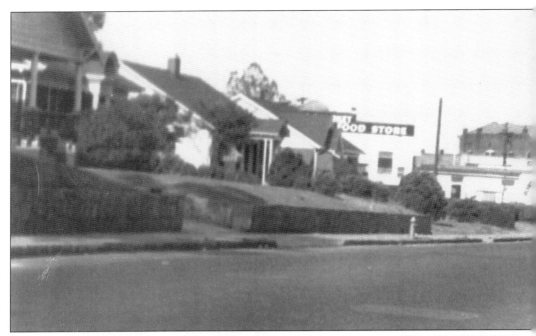

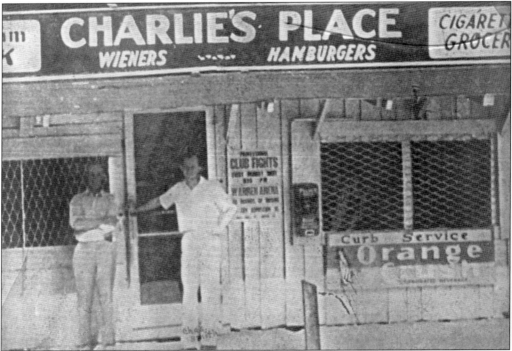

Charlie's Place was known for serving some of the best hamburgers in East Atlanta, which some attributed to Charles Smith (right) soaking the cooked patties in his mother's homemade, secret-recipe chili. Soldiers brought Coke bottles from around the world to add to the collection that lined the walls. Charlie's Place was first located on Moreland Avenue, and then at this location on Glenwood Avenue. (Courtesy of Martha Brown United Methodist Church.)

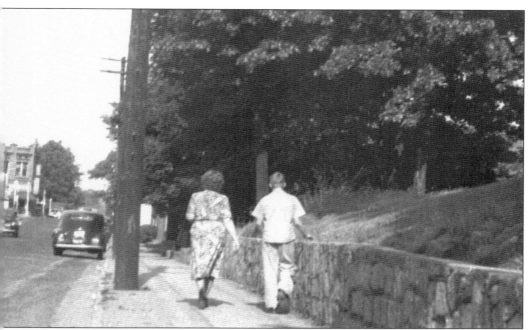

Many of the residences on Glenwood Avenue between Moreland and Flat Shoals Avenues were also being used as offices when this 1949 photograph was taken. Jim Arnold and his stepmother, Dee Arnold, walked along the wide sidewalks from their home in Ormewood Park to shop in East Atlanta. (Courtesy of Louis Arnold.)

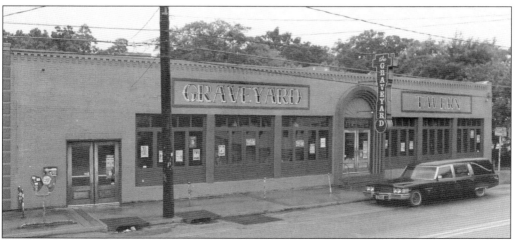

The Southern Feed Store was established in this building at Glenwood and Joseph Avenues in 1927. Williams Bros. Lumber expanded the building, adding a new facade for the Williams Refrigerator Corporation subsidiary that inhabited it from 1940 to 1942. The company built meat coolers using wood and shavings from the lumberyard planing mill as insulation. From 1944 to 1947, it was home to the Atlanta Dixie-Rush Bottling Company. In 2005, it became the Graveyard Tavern. (Photograph by Kristin Vanderpool.)

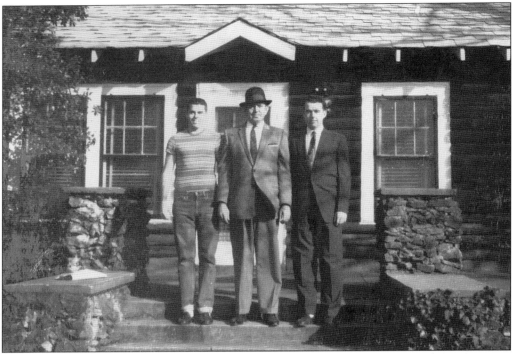

Dr. James F. Hackney, seen above between sons Larry (left) and Jimmy, lived with his family in this log cabin on Bouldercrest Drive. As seen below, Dr. Hackney, the Atlanta director of public health, was at the forefront of administering polio vaccines to children. As venereal disease became a serious problem in Atlanta, Dr. Hackney helped start the Venereal Disease Hospital and also worked with city and federal leaders to establish what would become the Centers for Disease Control. (Both courtesy of James E. Hackney.)

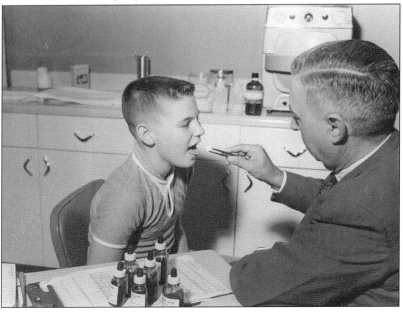

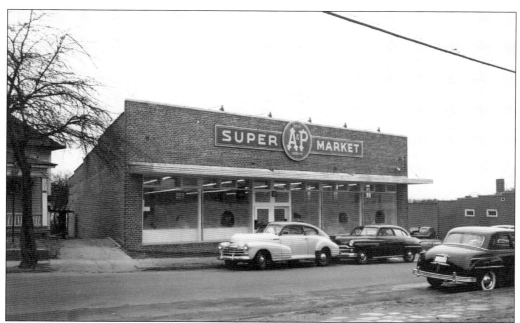

A&P Super Market opened at 470 Flat Shoals Avenue in 1949 and remained at this location through the 1970s. A smaller A&P grocery store had previously been located a few doors down at 486 Flat Shoals Avenue. (Courtesy of Georgia State University Special Collections and Archives.)

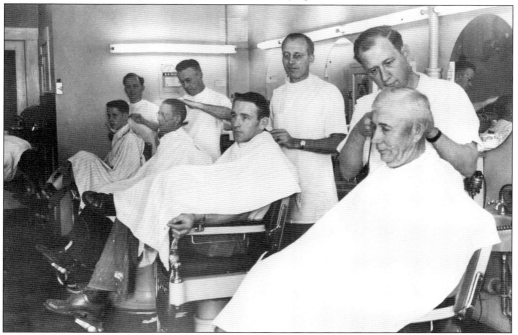

Some customers at the popular East Atlanta Barber Shop on Flat Shoals Avenue had a favorite barber, but there was little choice in who would cut their hair. In 1949, the barbers included (from left to right) Tom Long, Howard Pickins, and two unidentified men. (Courtesy of Martha Brown United Methodist Church.)

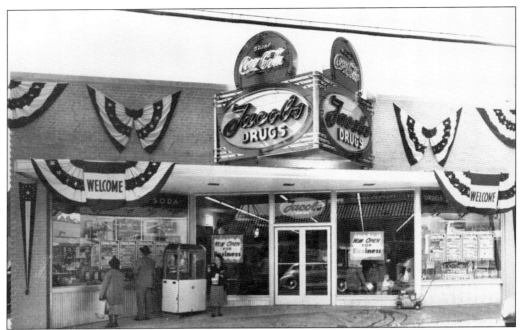

Jacob's Drugs opened an East Atlanta location in 1954, drawing customers with its Cherry Cokes and red booths. It also offered a free Coke to customers who bought their school supplies there. The original Jacob's Pharmacy was located in downtown Atlanta and was the first store to sell the new fountain drink Coca-Cola in 1886. (Courtesy of Georgia State University Special Collections and Archives.)

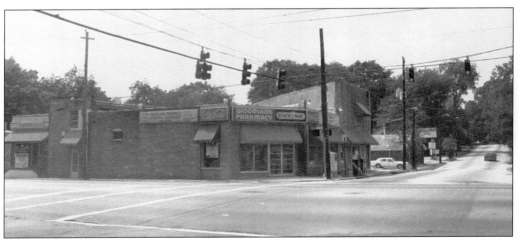

Woodland Pharmacy, seen here in the 1990s, opened on Woodland Avenue but relocated to the old Simpson's Grocery building at Moreland and Ormewood Avenues in the 1940s. Bill Elliott began working there as a bicycle delivery boy, and when Woodland's soda jerk left to fight in World War II, he was promoted to the prized fountain position. Elliot became the pharmacist and an owner in the 1950s, which he remained until 1996. (Courtesy of Bill and Janice Elliot.)

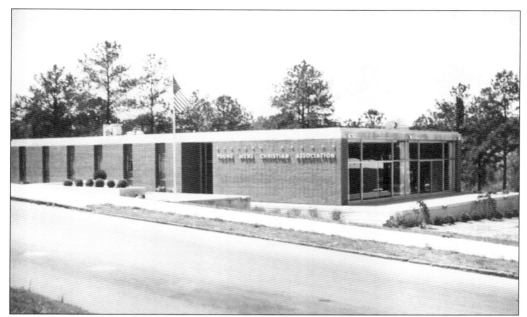

The YMCA built its southeast branch on Memorial Drive in 1959 at the site where the Battle of Atlanta began. What was originally called the eastern branch began in 1945, and, by 1952, it had an office above the East Atlanta Bank. The Memorial Drive building was demolished in 2012 to make way for a new YMCA Teen and Aquatic Center. (Courtesy of YMCA of Metro Atlanta.)

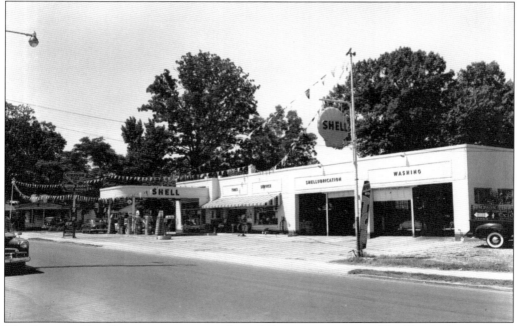

The Simpson Tire Company was a sprawling, full-service station on Flat Shoals Avenue near May Avenue when this photograph was taken in 1954. This building served as the Good Year Tire Center for many years and became the Midway Pub in 2008. (Courtesy of Georgia State University Special Collections and Archives.)

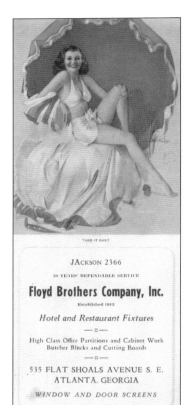

Floyd Brothers Company was one of East Atlanta's leading businesses. Located at 535 Flat Shoals Avenue, it was founded in the 1920s and manufactured high-end cabinets, bank and office fixtures, and other woodwork items. Below, a four-alarm fire swept through the Floyd Brothers Company building on December 22, 1952. Thousands of people reportedly jammed the streets to watch the firemen battle the blaze, one of the worst in Atlanta that year. It also caused damage to East Atlanta Pharmacy and East Atlanta Barber Shop. (Both courtesy of Mary Ann Hightower.)

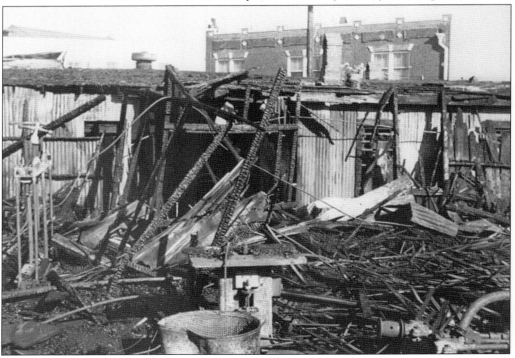

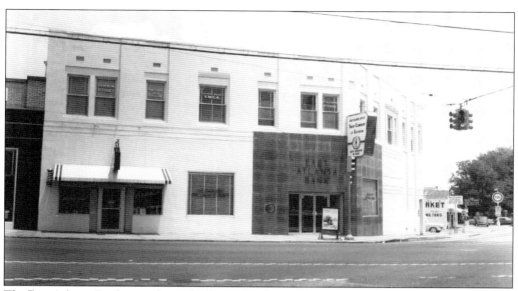

The East Atlanta Bank moved into the former Piggly Wiggly location in the 1950s after the building underwent a major renovation that included the removal of the parapets and the painting of the brick. The entrance received a sleek, mid-century design with the addition of stone veneer tiles. The interior was also renovated, with Floyd Brothers Company adding new woodwork and cabinetry throughout. Below, Hugh Rowland, vice president of the East Atlanta Bank, works at his desk in the enlarged bank lobby. Rowland was the nephew of bank president Malcolm Thompson, who began as a cashier in 1927 and worked his way up. (Above, courtesy of Georgia State University Special Collections and Archives; below, courtesy of Mary Ann Hightower.)

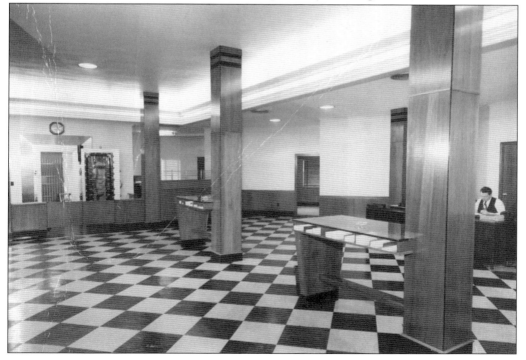

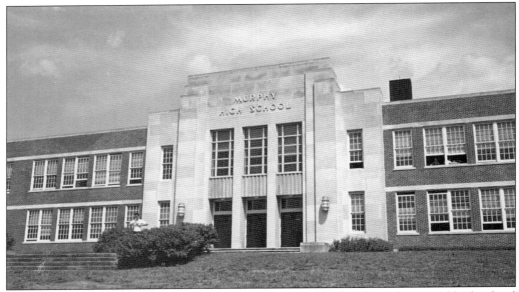

In 1946, Atlanta Public Schools decided to move to a neighborhood, coeducational high school concept due to overcrowding at Girls High School, Boys High School, and Tech High School, the three of which served the whole city. Murphy High School opened in 1948 on Clifton Street, serving grades eight through twelve. (Courtesy of Sherwood Harrington.)

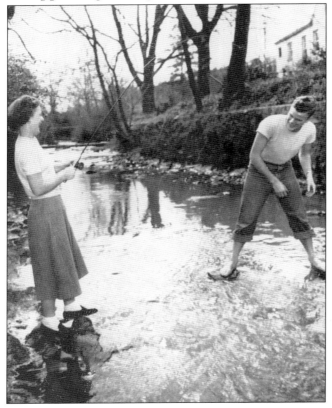

The 1949 choices for "Most Representative" at Murphy High School were Ann Callaway and Milford Bennett, who played it up in this *Azuwur* yearbook photograph in Sugar Creek. Within 10 years, the new Interstate 20 would alter this landscape. In the background on Clifton Street is the transmitter and facility for WAGA radio, one of only three stations located in Atlanta at that time. (Courtesy of the Atlanta Independent School System.)

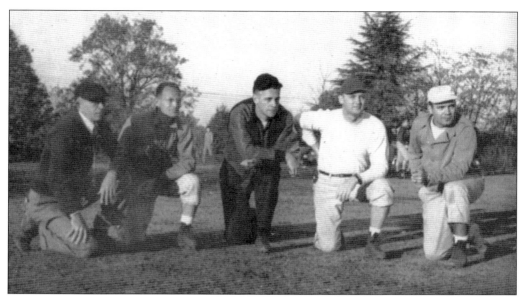

Joel Eaves (center) was the head football and basketball coach at Murphy High School after World War II. Coaching with him in 1948 were, from left to right, R.D. Powell, A.W. Patton, A.T. Harmon, and M.O. Phelps. In 1949, Eaves became the head basketball coach at Auburn University, where he never had a losing season. In 1963, he left to become the University of Georgia's athletic director, bringing with him young football coach Vince Dooley. (Courtesy of the Atlanta Independent School System.)

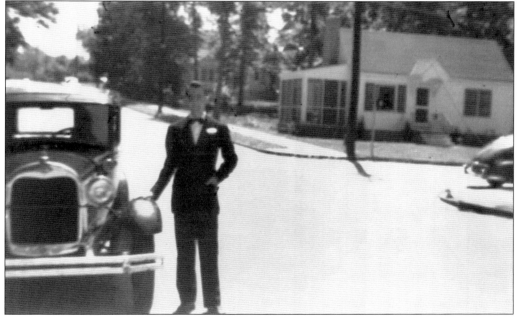

Murphy High School senior Marion Blackwell arrives in his 1929 Ford Model A automobile near Ormewood and Gresham Avenues to pick up his date, Laura Cronin, for the 1949 senior prom. Blackwell recalls being only one of four students at Murphy High School who owned an automobile at that time, with his being the best of the lot. (Courtesy of Marion Blackwell Jr.)

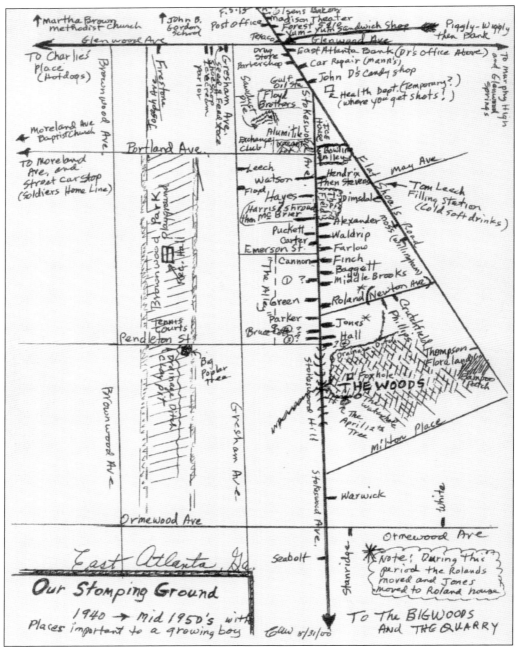

Many residents who lived in East Atlanta through the years recall it as the best place in the world to grow up. Carey Waldrip drew this map of his "stomping ground" in 2000 to highlight the places that were important to him as a boy during the 1940s and 1950s. (Courtesy of the Waldrip family.)

In 1955, Stephen Clarke dressed up as Peter Pan for Halloween trick-or-treating around his apartment complex, located off of Florida Avenue. These apartments were part of the postwar building boom in East Atlanta. (Courtesy of Donald Stephen Clarke.)

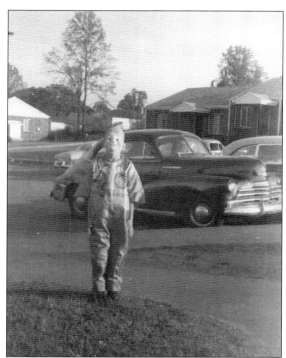

To celebrate their graduation from John B. Gordon Elementary School, the group of seventh-graders below dressed in costumes during Kids Day in 1956. Posing on the playground located behind Martha Brown United Methodist Church are, from left to right, (first row) Linda Parker and Billy Peacock; (second row) Bobby Crutchfield, Marie Porch, Jane Wilder, Faye Woodyard, Peggy Wofford, and Donna Lowery. (Courtesy of Lynn Giglio.)

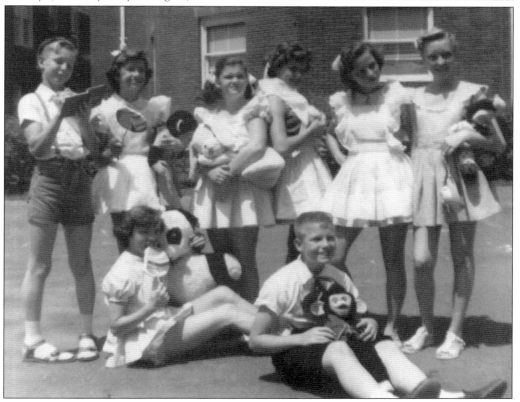

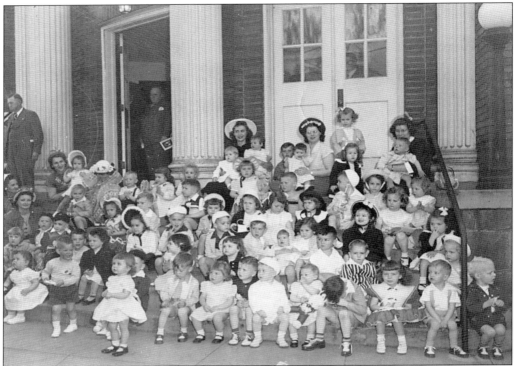

The growth and baby boom in East Atlanta after World War II was evident on Easter Sunday in 1951 at Martha Brown United Methodist Church. The church had an influx of 700 new members during this time and purchased more property for expansion. (Courtesy of Martha Brown United Methodist Church.)

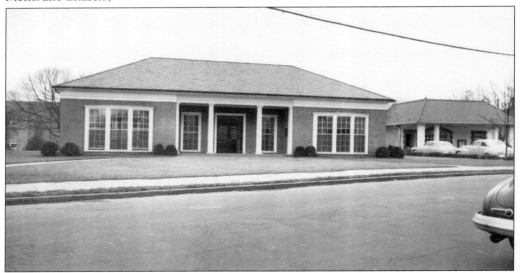

In 1949, East Atlanta received a new branch library at 457 Flat Shoals Avenue, next to the fire station, at a cost of about $48,000. A new branch library for African American patrons opened the following day on Hunter Street. This facility was enlarged in the 1970s to include two alcoves and a meeting room. (Courtesy of the Atlanta Fulton Public Library System.)

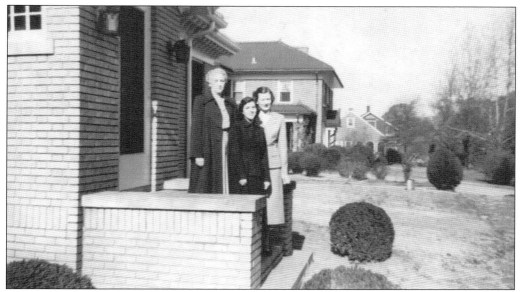

Sometimes referred to as "Millionaires Row," the homes along Flat Shoals Avenue south of Glenwood Avenue were owned by many prominent East Atlantans. Here, Beth Crabill (front) stands on her front steps at 721 Flat Shoals Avenue with her mother-in-law, Trudy Owens Crabill, and sister-in-law Betty Rogers. The homes in the background belonged to Dr. E.F. Fincher, grocer Charlie Everitt, and Madison Theatre owner George Gaston. (Courtesy of the Crabill family.)

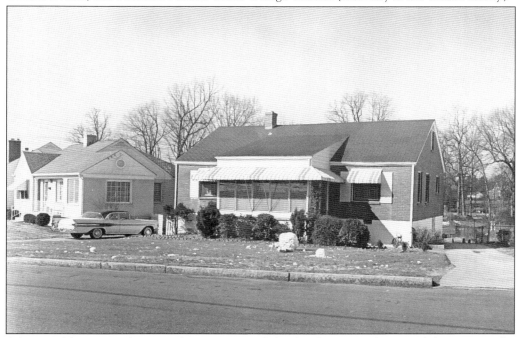

After World War II, a housing shortage spurred the development of more subdivisions in the area. The Tippens family home at 745 Blake Street, seen here in 1958, was typical of the small, affordable new bungalows being built in East Atlanta for returning GIs and their families. (Courtesy of the Tippens family.)

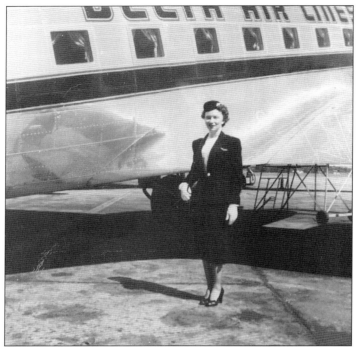

Many of East Atlanta's younger generation found new opportunities away from the area after the war. Joyce Matthews (left), who grew up on Van Epps Avenue, became a stewardess for Delta Airlines in 1948 before marrying her John B. Gordon Elementary School classmate Cuthbert "Bill" Pattillo. Below, Bill Pattillo (left) and his brother Charles "Buck" Pattillo (right) became two of the original members of the Thunderbirds, the first US Air Force official aerial demonstration team, in 1953. (Both courtesy of the Pattillo family.)

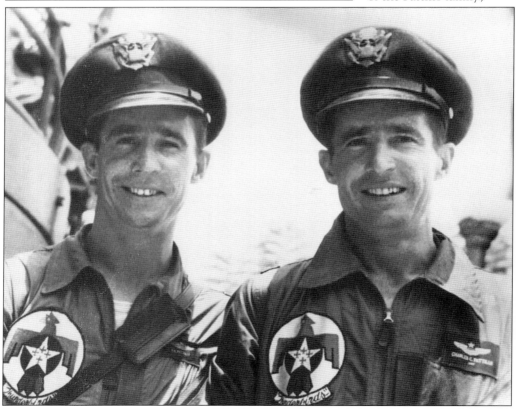

Five

DIVIDED BY THE INTERSTATE AND INTEGRATION

Two events threatened and challenged East Atlanta in the 1960s and 1970s. The first was the construction of Interstate 20, which severed Flat Shoals Avenue and other local street connections, isolating the community from neighborhoods to the north. Then, the Civil Rights Movement began to impact the area, bringing a fear of social change and prompting established white families to pull up their decades-old roots. Though many families stayed through the transition into a multiracial community, the neighborhood suffered economic decline. Unscrupulous and opportunistic real estate practices and the devaluation of property led to increased blight.

The quickly changing demographics were most apparent in the schools. East Atlanta High School was 70 percent white and 30 percent black in 1970. In 1971, the percentages were the exact opposite. Such quick transitions undermined the stability of the community. Some remaining white families enrolled their children in private schools. White churches struggled to remain in their East Atlanta buildings as their congregations began moving away. Many middle-class African American families moved to the neighborhood and assumed leadership roles. Lower property values also attracted lower-income and transient residents. As some white businesses closed down, African Americans established other successful businesses in their place. Rev. Willis Mitchell, a baker at Olson's Bakery, purchased that business in 1969, moved it across the street, and renamed it Willis' Bakery. It became the first African American business in East Atlanta.

Banks and some white businesses adapted to the transitions, though many commercial buildings remained vacant and fell into disrepair. The Madison Theatre, once the centerpiece of Flat Shoals Avenue, tried to adapt with the times, but, by the 1970s, it had become a mattress factory and warehouse. In the midst of the economic decline, East Atlanta appeared to have lost its identity. Suddenly, East Atlanta again sounded more like a direction from Atlanta instead of the vibrant, independent residential community and business district it had been.

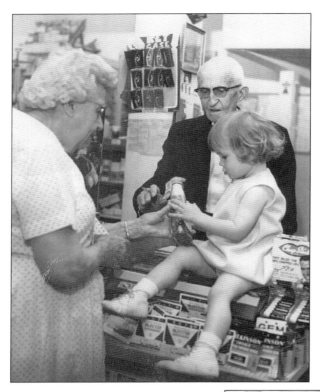

The small, locally owned pharmacies were still thriving in the 1960s. At left, Mary Lillie Floyd and her granddaughter Amy Hightower visit with Dr. Charles Hill, the longtime pharmacist at the East Atlanta Pharmacy. Dr. Hill was often referred to as East Atlanta's unofficial mayor. Bo Harper, whose father owned OK Drugs in the Madison Theatre building, and Jake Brown (below) began their pharmacist careers with Dr. Hill. In the 1960s, they opened Harper & Brown Pharmacy down the street. Brown later took it over, renaming it Brown's Pharmacy. (Left, courtesy of Mary Ann Hightower; below, photograph by Courtney Bryant.)

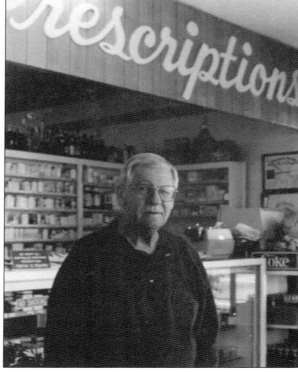

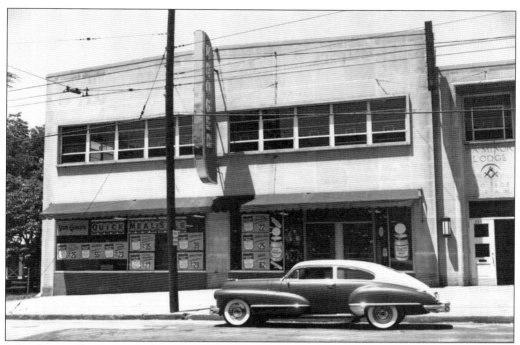

After having been in two locations on Flat Shoals Avenue, the E.A. Minor Masonic Lodge constructed a building at Moreland and Glenwood Avenues in 1948. At its peak in the late 1940s, the lodge reportedly had 1,700 members. In 1957, the first floor of the building was home to a Kroger. (Courtesy of Georgia State University Special Collections and Archives.)

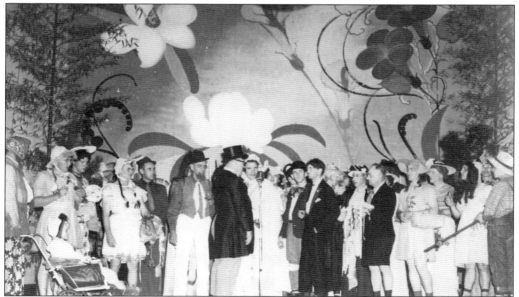

With a focus on family and bettering the community, the East Atlanta Exchange Club was a popular group that met on Gresham Avenue. Here, members present the Womanless Wedding, a fundraiser, probably held in the 1950s at Gordon Elementary School, in which men in drag played all the female characters. (Courtesy of Mary Ann Hightower.)

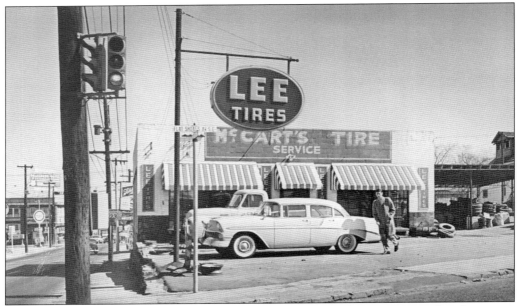

Flat Shoals Avenue at Memorial Drive was once a busy East Atlanta commercial and streetcar intersection. McCart's Tire Service was located on the southeast corner from the 1940s through the 1980s, in the former Jackson's Grocery. Over the decades, businesses at the intersection included other groceries, dry cleaners, drugstores, and barbershops. At one time, the Betsy Ross Lodge of the Ku Klux Klan met upstairs on the northeast corner. (Courtesy of the Tippens family.)

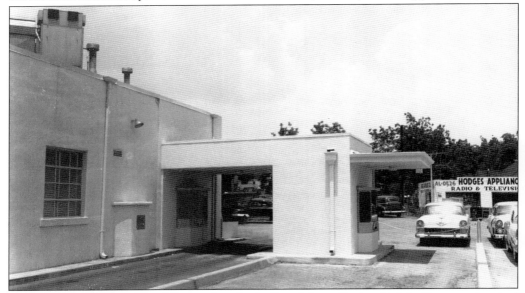

In 1956, the Trust Company of Georgia bought the East Atlanta Bank, which had been modernized with drive-through tellers. The new parent regional bank added its east-side headquarters on the second floor. In 1975, bank robbers tunneled from an adjacent building through two brick walls to reach the bank's vault. After the robbers triggered a silent alarm several times, authorities set a trap and foiled the attempt. (Courtesy of Georgia State University Special Collections and Archives.)

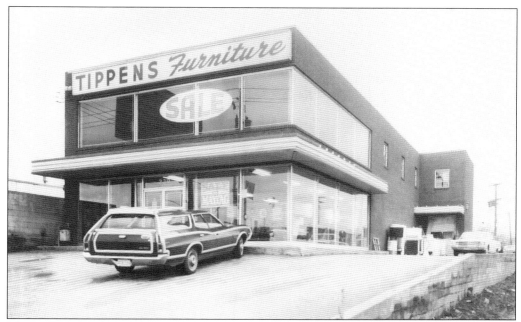

The Tippens family founded a furniture store in 1950, and it is one of the few businesses to survive through recent decades. They erected the building above at 229 Moreland Avenue in 1962. When the city changed its boundaries in 1976, making Interstate 20 the northern boundary of East Atlanta instead of Memorial Drive, Tippens Furniture was considered to be in Reynoldstown. The frame bungalow house below, at 205 Stovall Street, was also once considered part of East Atlanta. The large, stately home of East Atlanta pioneer John F. Faith was located a block away on Flat Shoals Avenue. (Both courtesy of the Tippens family.)

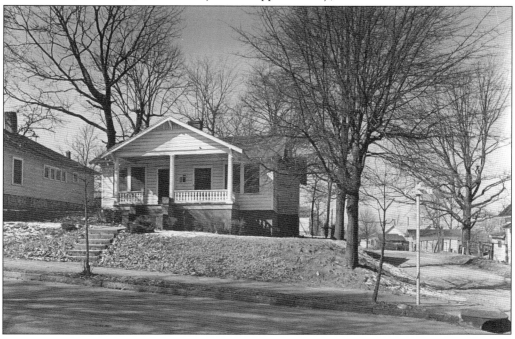

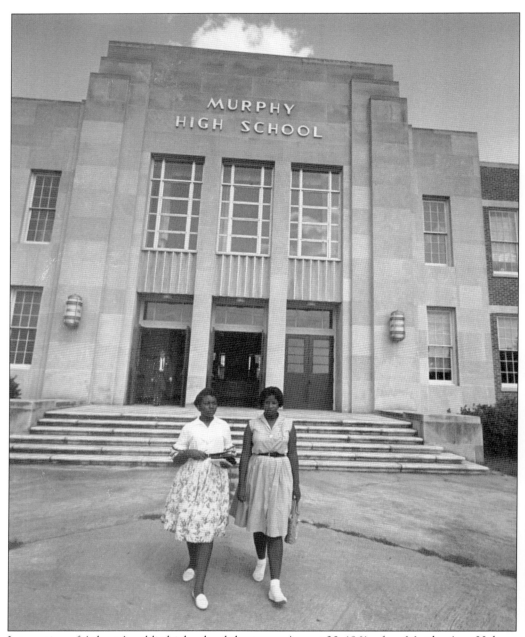

Integration of Atlanta's public high schools began on August 30, 1961, when Martha Ann Holmes (left) and Rosalyn Walton became the first African Americans to attend J.C. Murphy High School. The girls were two of the "Atlanta Nine," students attending African American schools who were handpicked for the integration of four of Atlanta's white high schools. To ensure their safety, the girls received police escorts to and from school for several months. In spite of racial tension in the city, there were no violent conflicts, only some verbal intimidation and a feeling of deep isolation from the rest of the student body. By the early 1970s, East Atlanta's schools were predominately African American. (Courtesy of Kenan Research Center at the Atlanta History Center.)

Former East Atlanta resident Herbert Jenkins was Atlanta's police chief from 1948 to 1973. He was committed to a peaceful transition during the civil rights–era desegregation and helped keep Atlanta from turning into another Little Rock. His parents moved to East Atlanta in 1924 and lived on Gresham Avenue. (Courtesy of the DeKalb History Center.)

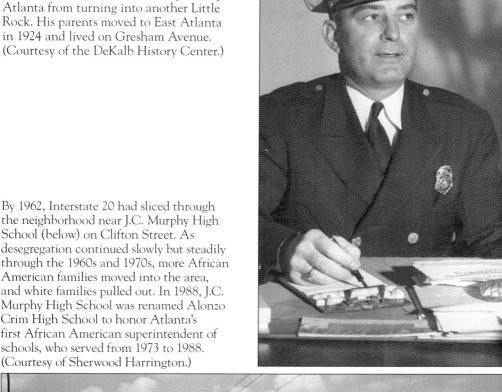

By 1962, Interstate 20 had sliced through the neighborhood near J.C. Murphy High School (below) on Clifton Street. As desegregation continued slowly but steadily through the 1960s and 1970s, more African American families moved into the area, and white families pulled out. In 1988, J.C. Murphy High School was renamed Alonzo Crim High School to honor Atlanta's first African American superintendent of schools, who served from 1973 to 1988. (Courtesy of Sherwood Harrington.)

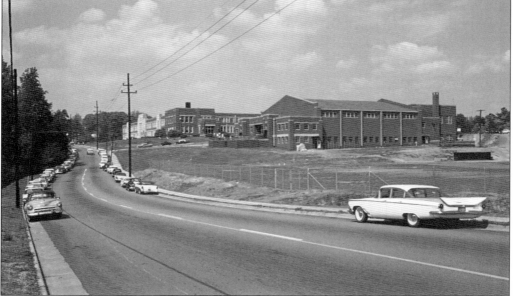

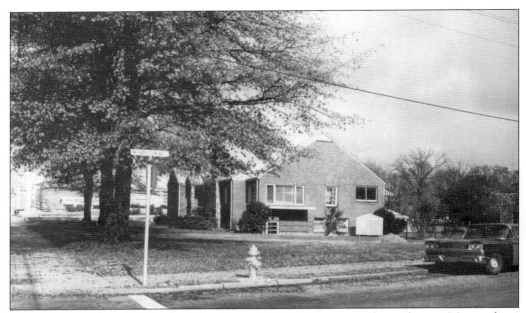

Martha Brown United Methodist Church turned its 1947 parsonage, located across Metropolitan Avenue, into its youth center. The house was eventually torn down for a parking lot and a Long John Silver's restaurant. Billionaire philanthropist J. Mack Robinson, who helped start the Yves Saint Laurent fashion house in the 1960s, grew up in a home located on this site in the 1920s and 1930s. (Courtesy of Martha Brown United Methodist Church.)

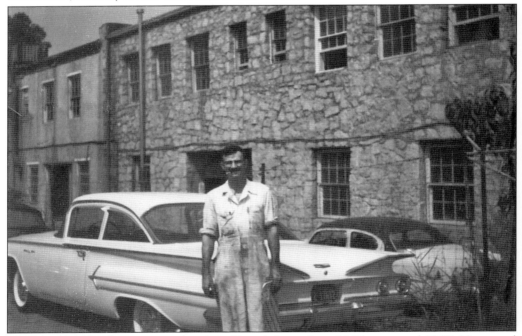

F.J. "Mac" McKnight was a mechanic in East Atlanta from 1946 to around 2000. He owned McKnight's Auto Service, located in the basement of the East Atlanta Furniture Store. The granite building had once been a carriage dealership. (Courtesy of Ann Lee Garbutt Bussey.)

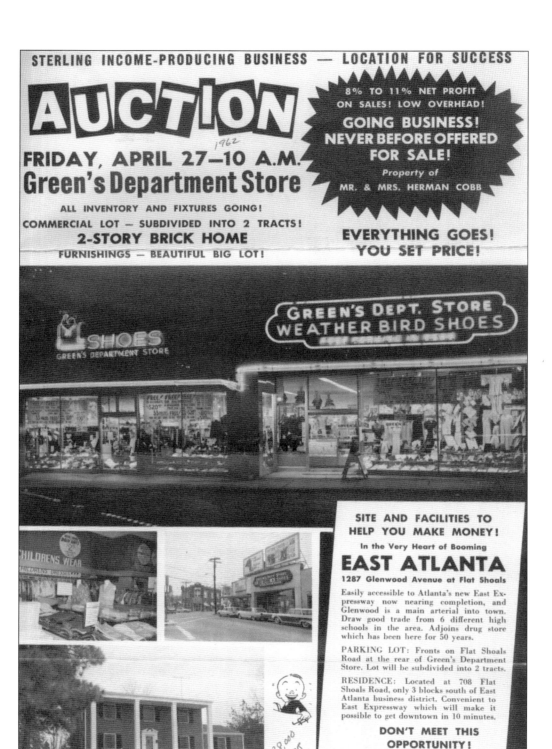

The East Atlanta Business District began changing significantly in the 1960s. Green's Department Store, located on the corner of Glenwood and Flat Shoals Avenues, sold its commercial lot, inventory, and fixtures at auction in 1962. (Courtesy of Louis Arnold.)

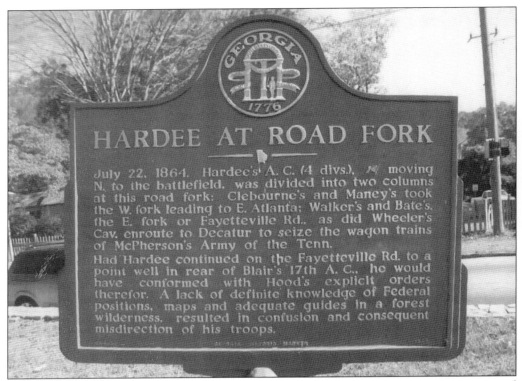

In 1964, the centennial celebration of the Battle of Atlanta and the Civil War in Georgia spurred the erection of markers throughout the city. More than 20 were placed in East Atlanta. This one was placed at Fayetteville Road and Bouldercrest Drive. (Courtesy of Henry Bryant.)

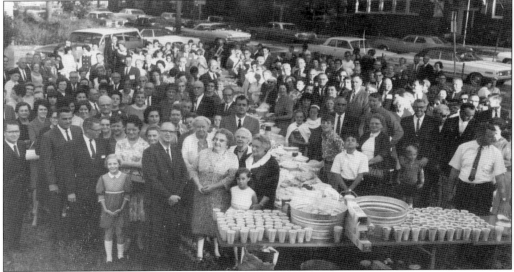

The 75th anniversary celebration of Martha Brown United Methodist Church in 1968 included a picnic on the lawn behind the youth center across from John B. Gordon Elementary School. Some members who had moved out of East Atlanta continued to return for church services and events for years. (Courtesy of Martha Brown United Methodist Church.)

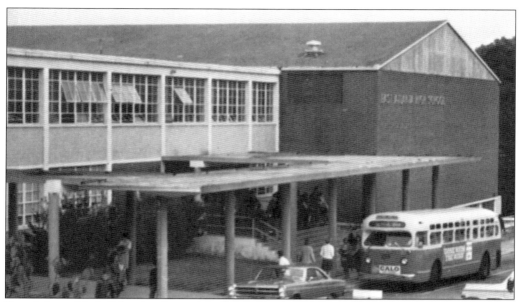

East Atlanta High School welcomed its first students in 1959, easing the crowded conditions at Murphy and Roosevelt High Schools. The school was built at the edge of East Atlanta on the old Hightower pasture land, perhaps anticipating further annexation of DeKalb County property by the City of Atlanta. When the photograph above was taken a decade later, the school was still predominately white. By 1972, as the yearbook photograph below of the student council shows, the racial demographics of the school and the neighborhood had dramatically changed. Two future Atlanta City Council members are in the photograph: Davetta Johnson (second row, third from left) and Natalyn Mosby Archibong (third row, far left). Archibong was copresident of the high school government that year. (Both courtesy of the Atlanta Independent School System.)

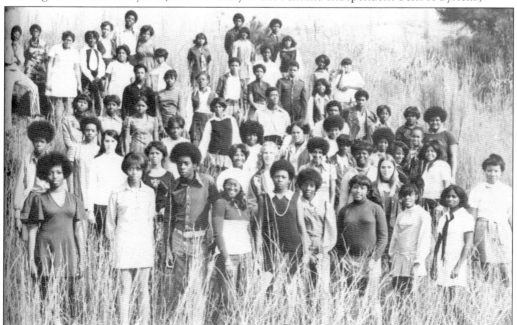

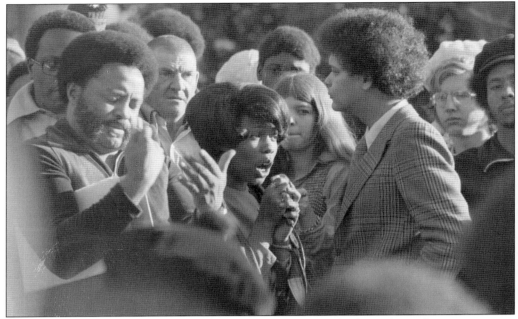

In 1973, East Atlantan Betty Clark (center foreground) became the first African American woman elected to the Georgia House of Representatives. In 1976, she spoke at this protest outside the state capitol in downtown Atlanta with civil rights leader and Georgia state representative Hosea Williams (left foreground) and Georgia state senator Julian Bond (right foreground). (Courtesy of Kenan Research Center at the Atlanta History Center.)

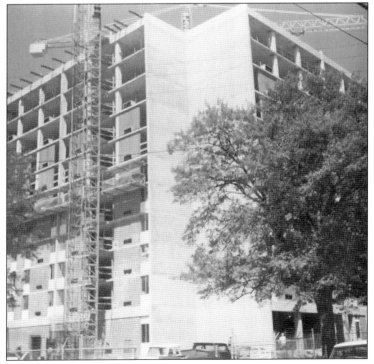

The tallest building in East Atlanta is the 11-story Branan Towers, seen here nearing completion on Glenwood Avenue in 1973. Martha Brown United Methodist Church sold land adjacent to the church to Wesley Woods for the purpose of constructing this retirement home for the aging community. (Courtesy of Wesley Woods Senior Living.)

Six

REBUILDING TOGETHER

By 1980, East Atlanta began attracting urban pioneers with its affordable housing and proximity to downtown. Among these adventurous newcomers were many gay people, who took a chance on the community for its accepting attitudes. Young professionals and families also began moving into the neighborhood, renovating the old houses and establishing an outpost of arts and creativity. The trickle of investors renovating and flipping houses for profit turned into a torrent after 2000.

Newcomers joined with existing residents—white and black—to form the East Atlanta Community Association, which advocated for quality of life while providing a means to actively work toward that goal. Neighborhood events were regularly held to promote the area as a welcoming place to live, work, and play. The *Porch Press*, founded in 1985, provided neighborhood news, binding the community together.

Residents and merchants tackled revitalization of the East Atlanta Business District, later rechristening it the "East Atlanta Village." Over the next two decades, two redevelopment plans were funded with federal grants to build two streetscape projects in five phases. Investors like Don Bender and Booker Rashaad purchased commercial buildings and then brought them up to code using federal loans and private funds. Federal monies also rebuilt Brownwood Park's aging structures. When the East Atlanta Library was closing in the early 1980s due to consolidation of city and county services, residents mounted a statewide special tax referendum to provide for the library's future and then lobbied for a new library in the East Atlanta Village.

When the Olympic torch came through East Atlanta in 1996, it again became the recognized center of southeast Atlanta when a vibrant, diverse crowd lined its avenues and persistently remained through the night for the historic passing. It was the kind of scene leaders of this period envisioned when they created the slogan "Uniquely East Atlanta" to describe what East Atlanta was becoming.

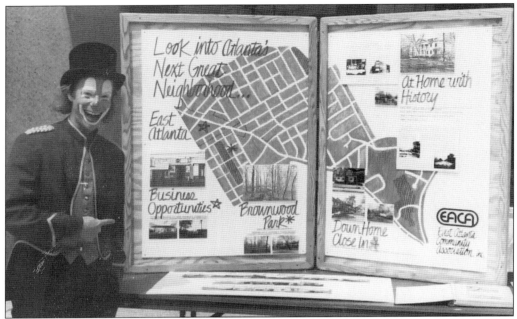

The East Atlanta Community Association participated in a city festival of neighborhoods in midtown in 1980 when the North Avenue MARTA (Metropolitan Atlanta Rapid Transit Authority) opened. Association president Tom Johnson, dressed as a clown, reintroduced East Atlanta as "Atlanta's next great neighborhood." City planning director Panke Bradley visited the booth and offered help with redevelopment. The display backdrop included a street map of East Atlanta, which resembled a fish. (Courtesy of Henry Bryant.)

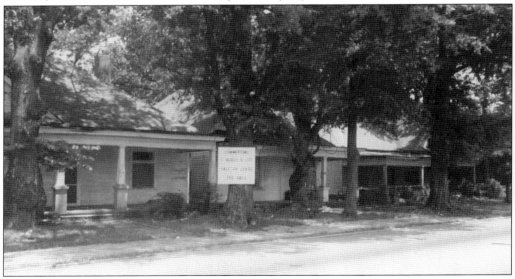

These structures on Flat Shoals Avenue near Oak Grove Avenue were three of the last remaining residential buildings in the East Atlanta Business District when a city-development study was launched in the early 1980s. Marketed for commercial use, they soon became day care centers and an antique shop. The two on the left were destroyed in a 2008 tornado. (Photograph by Henry Bryant.)

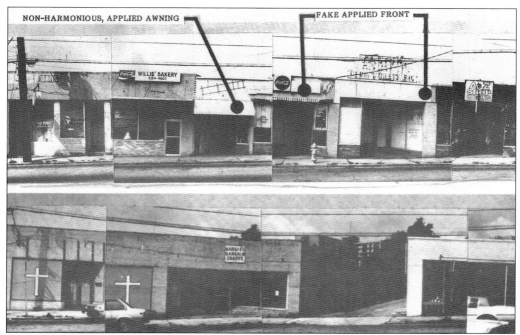

This series of 35-millimeter photographs glued together partially recreated the west side of Flat Shoals Avenue between Metropolitan and Glenwood Avenues. The montage with critical notation was part of the Atlanta Planning Department's East Atlanta study, completed in 1983. Willis' Bakery had survived, but 60 percent of the commercial space was either vacant or being used for storefront churches or used-tire storage. (Courtesy of Henry Bryant.)

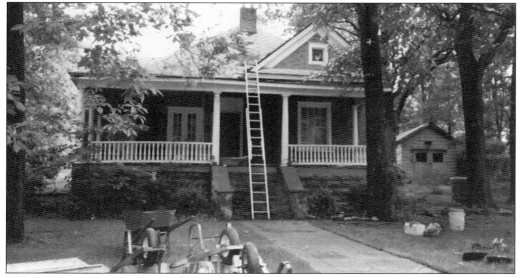

Older residences surrounding the business district were beginning to be renovated by 1983. Charles B. Everitt built this home at 1340 Metropolitan Avenue for his family in 1906 when they moved off of the busy Flat Shoals highway. Although only lived in by three families, the home was due for restoration and updating by the Bryant family, who moved there in 1980. (Photograph by Henry Bryant.)

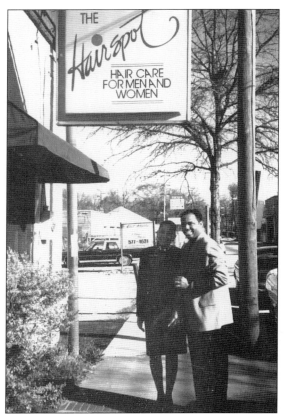

Dorothy Rose (left) was the owner of one of the first new businesses to open as redevelopment began in the East Atlanta Business District. She founded The Hairspot in the old East Atlanta Bank building and then moved to 534 Flat Shoals Avenue. Her son, Juan, (right) began sweeping floors there as a child and grew up to run the business. Rose helped to get block grant monies for the new streetscape seen here. (Courtesy of Dorothy Rose.)

An African American–owned business that came as a direct result of redevelopment efforts was the East Atlanta Dental Care Center (below), owned by Dr. Arlene Lester and her brother Dr. Jack Lester. The building, located at 440 Flat Shoals Avenue, was originally built for Liberty Mutual Insurance Company in the 1950s and was easily adapted into a first-class dental office. (Photograph by Henry Bryant.)

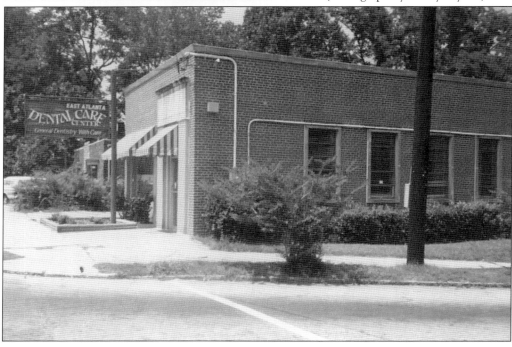

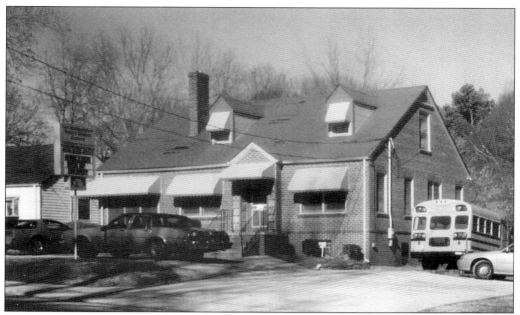

The Flat Shoals Child Development Center, on Flat Shoals Avenue near Bouldercrest Drive, was founded in a residential structure years before redevelopment started. African American owner Evelyn Bailey was one of the neighborhood leaders who lobbied for Community Development Block Grant funds and federal loans for East Atlanta in the 1980s. (Courtesy of Evelyn Bailey.)

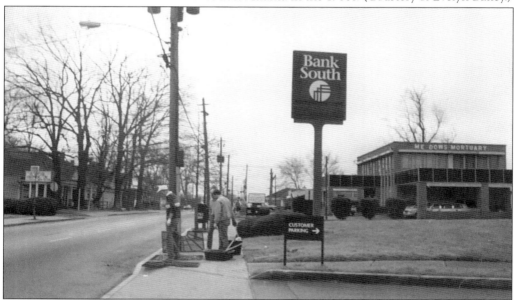

The East Atlanta study highlighted the prevalence of locally owned property in the business district and surrounding area, as well as the presence of four banks and a dozen real estate and insurance companies—all indicators of economic health. The area showed more vitality with new Asian American and African American businesses, like Meadows Mortuary, which occupied the former Gulf Life Insurance Company district headquarters on Flat Shoals Avenue. (Photograph by Henry Bryant.)

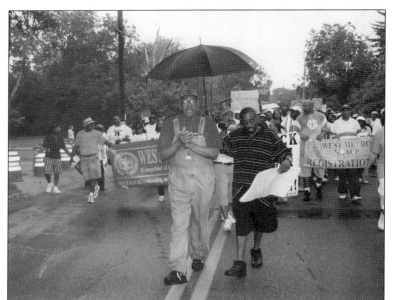

John Evans, DeKalb NAACP president (in overalls), was elected DeKalb County's first African American county commissioner in 1982. He was also a member of the MARTA Board of Directors and once played in the Negro Baseball League. He and his wife, former Atlanta School Board member Ina Evans, lived on Bouldercrest Drive. (Courtesy of Ina Evans.)

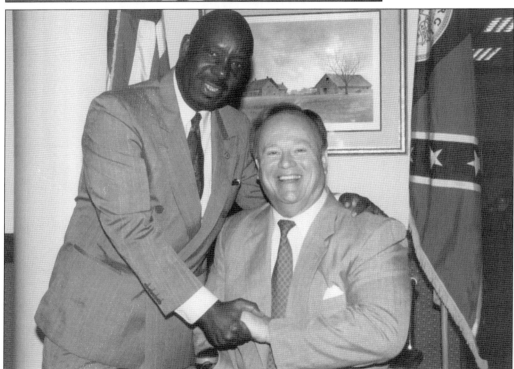

Nathanial "Nate" Mosby, seen here on the left with Georgia secretary of state Max Cleland in 1994, became the second African American elected to the DeKalb County Commission. The Mosby family moved to East Atlanta in 1968. Mosby's wife, Gwendolyn, taught at Burgess Elementary School. In 2002, their son Howard was elected to the Georgia House of Representatives, and their daughter Natalyn was elected as the Atlanta City Council's District 5 representative. (Courtesy of the Mosby family.)

The East Atlanta Community Association began a neighborhood festival in 1982 to promote the area as a diverse and friendly place to live, work, and play near the amenities of the city. The event, in Brownwood Park, featured five hours of musical entertainment, a children's activity area, a parade, arts and crafts, a hamburger cookout, and a Battle of Atlanta tour. It continued annually for 13 years. (Courtesy of Henry Bryant.)

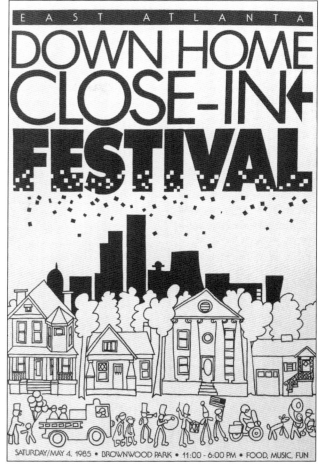

Below, in November 1989, Masjid of Al-Islam led a walk against crime and drugs through the East Atlanta Village. Many members of the mosque, located on nearby Fayetteville Road, not only had businesses in the East Atlanta Business District but also lived in the neighborhood. Imam Plemon El-Amin resided on Flat Shoals Avenue. (Courtesy of Plemon El-Amin.)

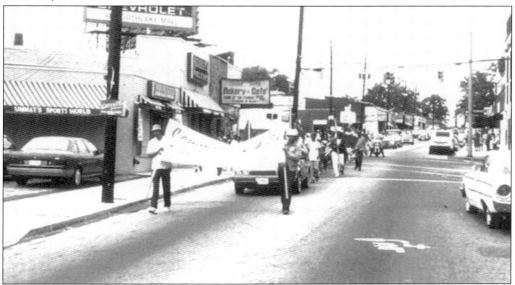

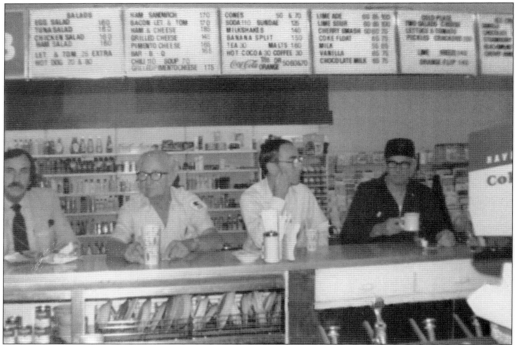

For decades, the lunch counter in the center of Woodland Pharmacy drew neighborhood regulars, such as these diners. Gov. Joe Frank Harris even came from the capitol in the 1980s. The cherry and lime smashes and pimento cheese sandwiches were always in demand. The pharmacy was bought out by a national chain in the 1990s. The building was later demolished to build a Little Azio pizza restaurant. (Courtesy of Bill and Janice Elliot.)

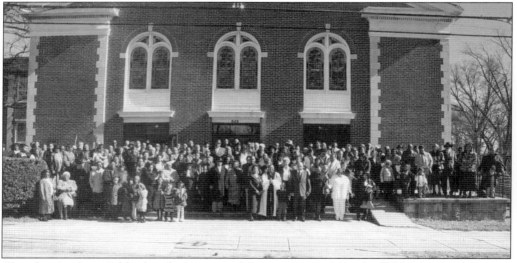

Churches in the neighborhood were part of the racial transition. In 1989, Moreland Avenue Baptist Church sold its property to First Iconium Baptist Church. Rev. Timothy McDonald III, the leader of the Concerned Black Clergy, led First Iconium Baptist Church in its move from Atlanta's West End to East Atlanta. Here, members pose on the steps along Moreland Avenue in 2012. (Courtesy of First Iconium Baptist Church.)

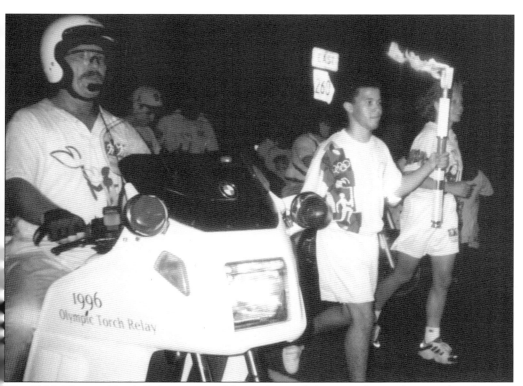

The 1996 Olympic Torch Relay was a red-letter day in Atlanta as the torch arrived and took a circuitous route across the city. It was scheduled to arrive in East Atlanta at 2:45 a.m. but did not get to Flat Shoals and Glenwood Avenues (above) until nearly sunrise. Area residents lined the streets all night, and several new businesses, including Heaping Bowl & Brew, Grant Central Pizza, and Sacred Grounds Café, stayed open to serve the crowds. A new day in East Atlanta had dawned. The Zuber-Jarrell House flung open its doors for an all-night house party, inviting curious neighbors, many of whom had never been inside. The house had recently been placed in the National Register and opened as a bed-and-breakfast. (Above, photograph by Genie Strickland; below, courtesy of Evelyn Bailey.)

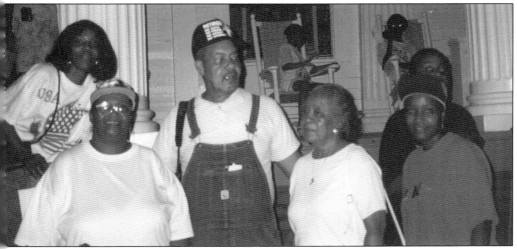

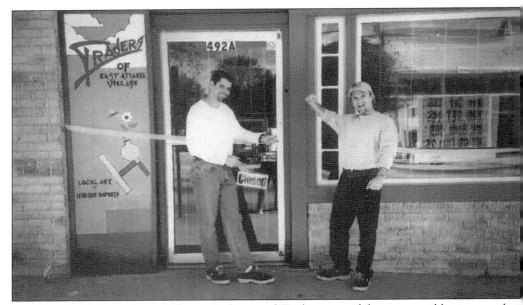

Partners Michael Knight and Shawn Ergle owned Traders, one of the new retail businesses that opened on Flat Shoals Avenue. They continued the long tradition of business owners living and working in East Atlanta. Specializing in fun gift products and housewares, Traders had quadrupled in size by 2000 and moved to the west side of the street to add designer furnishings to its list of products. Knight later continued it as Kaboodle. (Courtesy of Michael Knight.)

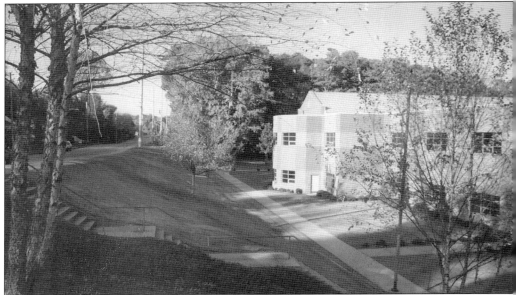

H.O. Burgess Elementary School, on Clifton Avenue, and Gartha Peterson Elementary School, on Mary Dell Avenue, merged to form Burgess-Peterson Academy. The old Burgess building was demolished and replaced by a new building in 2004. This view looks north along the Clifton Street schoolyard. It is one of Atlanta's highest-performing elementary schools. In 2011, First Lady Michelle Obama visited the school, praising its emphasis on health and nutrition. (Photograph by Henry Bryant.)

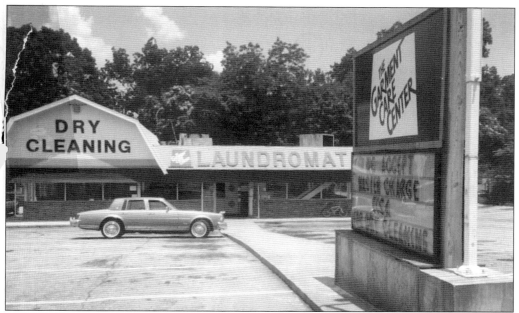

Jim Busby established a coin Laundromat and dry cleaner at the corner of Flat Shoals and McPherson Avenues in the old Dairy Queen, built in the 1960s. Busby, one of the founders of the East Atlanta Business Association, partnered with 36 area residents to purchase the East Atlanta Hardware Store in 1989. The Dairy Queen building was demolished to make way for the new library construction in 2004. The library became Fulton County's first LEED (Leadership in Energy and Environmental Design) building. It was also the first new construction in the East Atlanta Village to conform to neighborhood commercial zoning. (Above, photograph by Henry Bryant; below, courtesy of the Atlanta Fulton Public Library System.)

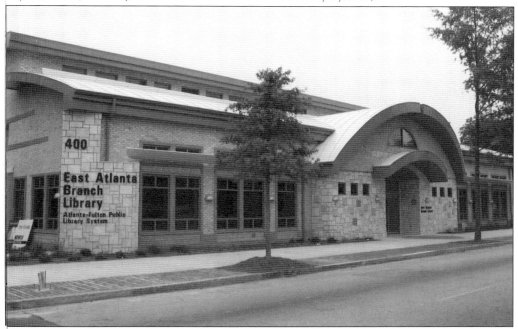

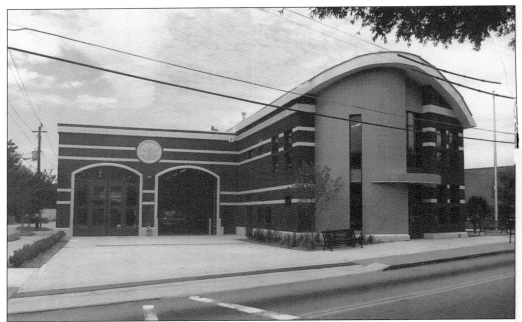

Fire Station No. 13, with its cloverleaf insignia, moved across Metropolitan Avenue to a new building on Flat Shoals Avenue in 2007. This two-story structure featured many modern amenities as well as an old-fashioned brass pole for fast response to emergencies from the second floor and dual drive-through bays for its pumper truck. (Photograph by Henry Bryant.)

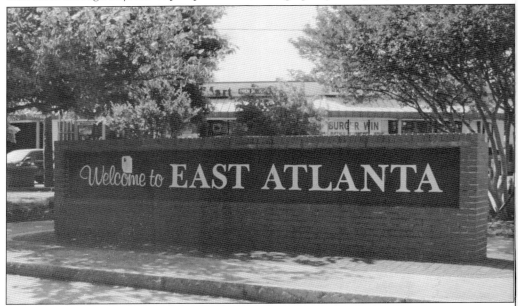

The "Welcome to East Atlanta" sign at the Moreland and Flat Shoals Avenues entrance was constructed in the 1980s as part of the streetscape improvements. It was part of a comprehensive effort to establish community identity, and the East Atlanta Business District soon became known as the East Atlanta Village, or the EAV. The sign became a landmark but was eventually replaced in 2013. (Photograph by David VanCronkhite.)

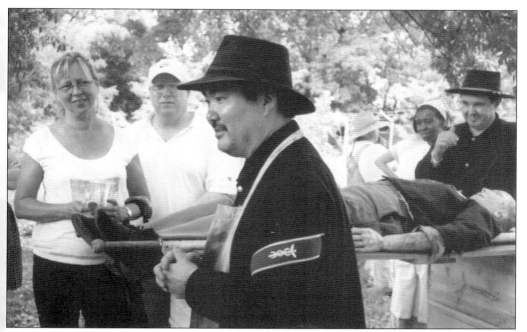

The Battle of Atlanta Commemoration Organization (BATL) began in Brownwood Park in 2003 to commemorate the historic Battle of Atlanta. This living-history encampment in the East Atlanta Village in 2004 featured a portrayal of a Union army medical officer by East Atlanta resident David Furukawa. Troops were positioned in the playground of the closed Gordon Elementary School, which is along the front lines of the Civil War battle. (Courtesy of BATL.)

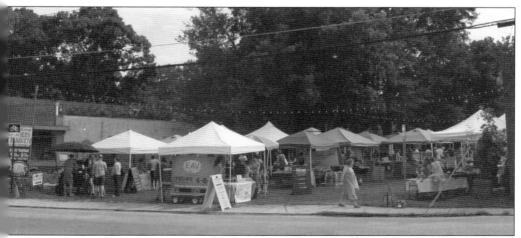

Following in the long tradition of East Atlanta's neighborhood grocers and truck farms, the East Atlanta Farmers Market was established to provide local sustainability and a stronger local food system. The market, open on Thursdays from April to December, moved to several locations before finding a home on Flat Shoals Avenue near the location of the 1877 Traveler's Rest Baptist Church. (Photograph by Kristin Vanderpool.)

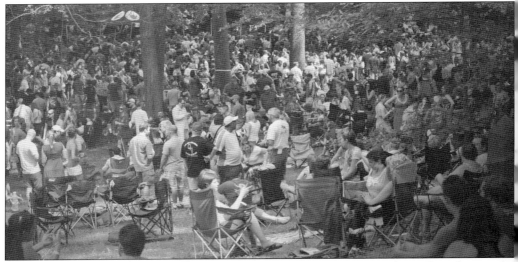

The East Atlanta Beer Festival is the major fundraiser for the East Atlanta Foundation, the largest funder of community projects in and around the area. It began in 2004 on the grounds of the old J.B. Gordon Elementary School and moved to Brownwood Park in 2011. Thousands from the Atlanta metropolitan area have attended to taste the craft beers and enjoy the local food and music. (Photograph by Mark Lin.)

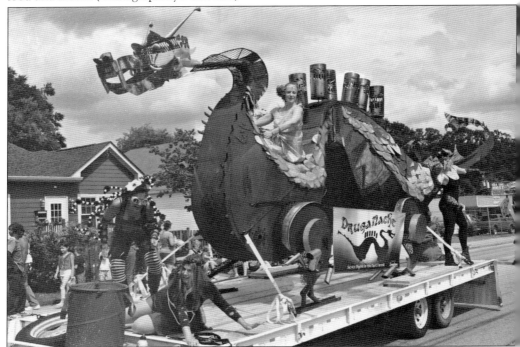

The EAV Strut was organized in 1999 to promote the neighborhood and local businesses with an eclectic parade, music performances, a book sale, children's activities, an artists' market, and even a circus. This 2012 parade float promoted *DrugaNacht*, an outdoor drama held in Brownwood Park. This *Dragon of Compassion* sculpture, created by Ryan Mathern, found its permanent home in East Atlanta. (Photograph by Krissy Venneman.)

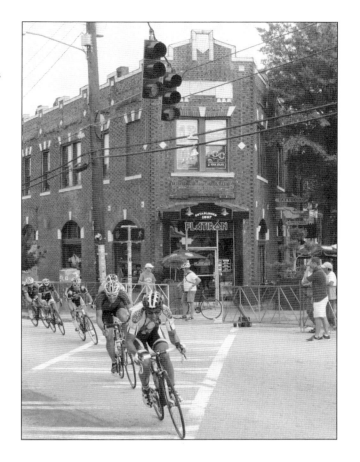

The 1911 East Atlanta Bank building has remained the landmark of the neighborhood for more than 100 years and has continued to be the backdrop for new events, including the inaugural Litespeed BMW Criterium cycling race in 2012. (Photograph by David VanCronkhite.)

BIBLIOGRAPHY

Bryant, Henry and Wayne Carey. *The Battle of Atlanta Monuments: Historic Resource Research and Analysis.* Atlanta: Bryant Art Direction, 2012.

Carson, O.E. *The Trolley Titans: A Mobile History of Atlanta.* Glendale, CA: Interurban Press, 1981.

Gaddis, Charles. *Roses in December, 1930–1992: A History of Martha Brown Methodist Church and East Atlanta.* East Atlanta, GA: Martha Brown United Methodist Church, 1992.

Garrett, Franklin M. *Atlanta and Environs,* vols. 1 and 2. Athens, GA: University of Georgia Press, 1954, 1969, 1988.

Martin, Harold M. *Atlanta and Environs,* vol. 3. Athens, GA: University of Georgia Press, 1987.

Price, Vivian. *The History of DeKalb County, Georgia, 1822–1900.* Fernandina Beach, FL: Wolfe Publishing Company, 1997.

Discover Thousands of Local History Books Featuring Millions of Vintage Images

Arcadia Publishing, the leading local history publisher in the United States, is committed to making history accessible and meaningful through publishing books that celebrate and preserve the heritage of America's people and places.

Find more books like this at
www.arcadiapublishing.com

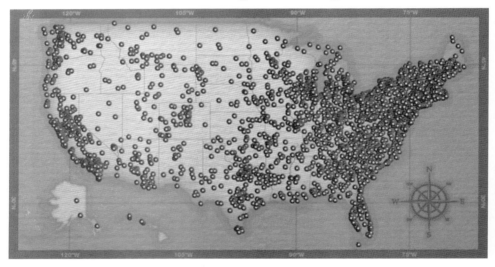

Search for your hometown history, your old stomping grounds, and even your favorite sports team.

Consistent with our mission to preserve history on a local level, this book was printed in South Carolina on American-made paper and manufactured entirely in the United States. Products carrying the accredited Forest Stewardship Council (FSC) label are printed on 100 percent FSC-certified paper.

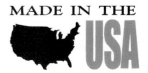